Blue Pyramids

Published by ECW PRESS
2120 Queen Street East, Suite 200, Toronto, Ontario, Canada M4E 1E2

NATIONAL LIBRARY OF CANADA CATALOGUING IN PUBLICATION DATA

Priest, Robert, 1951–
Blue pyramids: new and selected poems / Robert Priest.
Poems.
A misFit Book

ISBN 1-55022-554-5

1. Title.

PS8581.R47B58 2002   C811'.54   C2002-902212-6
PR9199.3.P745B58 2002

A misFit book edited by Michael Holmes
Cover and Text Design: Darren Holmes
Production and Typesetting: Mary Bowness
Printing: Transcontinental

This book is set in Bembo and Avant Garde

The publication of *Blue Pyramids* has been generously supported by the Canada Council, the Ontario Arts Council, and the Government of Canada through the Book Publishing Industry Development Program. Canada

DISTRIBUTION
CANADA: Jaguar Book Group, 100 Armstrong Avenue, Georgetown, ON L7G 5S4

PRINTED AND BOUND IN CANADA

ECW PRESS
ecwpress.com

Robert Priest

Blue Pyramids

New and Selected Poems

ecw press

CONTENTS

To my beloved Marsha

ACKNOWLEDGEMENTS

Over the past 30 years, many of these poems have appeared in numerous publications, including the following books: *The Visible Man* (Unfinished Monument Press, 1979), *Sadness of Spacemen* (Dreadnaught Press, 1980), *The Man who broke out of the Letter X* (Coach House Press, 1984), *The Mad Hand* (Coach House Press, 1988), *Scream Blue Living* (The Mercury Press, 1992), *Resurrection in the Cartoon* (ECW Press, 1997), and *The Time Release Poems* (EKSTASIS, 1998).

Thanks to the editors of those books: Albert Moritz, Linda Davey, Christopher Dewdney, Bev Daurio, Michael Holmes, and Richard Olafsun.

The author also gratefully acknowledges the financial assistance of: The Canada Council for the Arts, The Ontario Arts Council and the Toronto Arts Council.

Thanks also to: Mendelson Joe, Allen Booth, Marsha Kirzner, my parents, my brother and sister — and to my children.

In memory of: Libby Scheier, Linda Davey, Ted Plantos, Srul Irving Glik, and Derrick Ilsey.

Some of these poems are available as videos online at: www.poempainter.com.

Blue Pyramids is Volume 1 of *Phormacopia*. Volume II: *New and Selected Prose Poems* will be published next year.

CRUMBS

one crumb is a hook
to another crumb

and you can never go anywhere
but to another crumb
and there are advertisements on the way
all for a "better" crumb

and you can never have
the whole loaf

WHAT UGLY IS

i put on a man mask
and went among the people of earth
in search of what
ugly
means

many years the word had troubled
me, as i listened
over and over
to some of the approximately
four billion
mouth sounds
which these
animals
make

beauty i had come to understand
in stars
in eyes
the silver lapping of the oceans there
but ugly
what did it mean?

unrecognized
never speaking
but always listening
i walked their streets
and cities
i went into their starvations
their working places
deep in mines
i climbed a mountain
and looked into the writings

and holy codes
of their artists
but it wasn't until
i shared quarters with an actual family
and watched in shock
the upbringing of their young
that i realized
ugly
is what happens to something
you don't love
enough

ON GENUFLECTION

and in buildings huge enough
to house dinosaurs
they worship a creature so small
that they have to get down on their knees
  to talk to him

INCARNATION

have a place for me
a perfect fit
make me one with my need
pour the warm light liquid
all down my naked body
i have a genetic expectation
a feeling for arrival
i'm coming down
like a thousand birds onto the black branch
i'm coming down
a zeppelin, a bag of blue air
into the tree-shaped brains
into the dendrite forest
into the longing cell
i have toes for my toes
and nose for my nose
i'm coming down into my liver
descending into my lungs
i am diving down into the cold
black waters of the belly
a million miles into my stomach
and i still have not rung
the bottom's deep belltone
i am drifting down in mind's vines
into clear blue bones
into the orange skull, the blind gristle
in pulses of pure black soul
through a long rubber tube
through a bronze body
on a reel
on an anchor long since sunk
in the never-to-be-shaken bottom of me
to the blackened tree

mind cross
joining place
to the socket
in the riverbed
the pierced Cartesian crossroad
with a stitch of uncuttable time
i am coming down
like the entire airforce
onto the black ship
i am coming down like the monarchs on Mexico

the body is a vast tropic
unreachable by foot
i am lost between volcanoes
there are a thousand miles of air
above my head
in a moment more
a second more
my feet will touch the ground
and my feet
are the ground
my eyes are the light
the air breathes me in
and exhales me in a long fluttering flow
i am down in my body
like the liquid rains
like the finally fallen peak
the obese suspended Buddhas
the plutonium Christs with their tears of heavy water
i am down with my jade-grown bones
my spirit legs bicycling
and the earth touches me
like a forever denied son
like an exile returned illegally
the earth touches me like a long lost mother
and her name is terra

terror
her name is life

BIRTH

nothing is ordained
  the infant stifling in the cot
  does not predict
  veins rising
  through an ancient hand
the child upon the pendulum
  hooting for joy
  predicts nothing

the past at least is certain

i am face to face
  with my origin
  my mother's grim face
her sweat upon the pillow
the long-forgotten house of blood
forever closed to me

on this cold hearth
writing in the oracle of the scar
i speak my first shrill prophecy

SLIGHT EXAGGERATION OF A CHILDHOOD INCIDENT

when i was two
a garbage man gave me a trumpet

it was a small silver
winding dirty trumpet

and shrieking at my own thunder
like any other prodigy mad with energy

i bellowed down Thames Street
levelling buildings, knocking down churches

with my blasts, of course the neighbours
complained, prodigy or no prodigy

they were having no such slumbers
as their very precious own

disturbed by little manic urchins
such as i was

but my mother in her arrogant way
defied them and sat severely on the porch

watching with pride my short pants parade
go boastfully by

it was the police finally
who had to silence me

arriving on bicycles with bells
and blowing whistles

i was standing on a post
in a circle of my peers

and when the bobby said
"eaaah ooze makin' oowl 'at noise 'en?"

the circle opened magically before me
and they all pointed and said

"it's him —
it's little Robert Priest."

EDUCATION OF SHIT

After he was shit
The shit
Went to shit school
In order to learn
How better
To be shit
For years and years he studied
Coming closer and closer
To his degree in shit —
His doctorate in crap —
Learning to be shit
Learning to be shit
One day you will be shit
People will see you and call you shit
They will call you turd
Diarrhoetic eyeball, potty, poop
Splatter mouth
One day you will stand up tall
And know that you are excrement —
A fully trained faece
One day you will have a slip of paper
That tells you what you are —

A complete piece of shit!

AN ADVANTAGE OF THE IDENTITY CRISIS

you may remember me
I was the great idealist
I wandered all the world with a bag of filth
and anyone I met I said — here
take whatever you think is your rightful share
well all I got for my troubles was a face full of spit
so, disillusioned with the backward generosity of men
I took to saying
fuck fuck fuck
over and over again as though it were a password
that might make someone let me in somewhere
so they threw me in a six foot cell
with sixteen other guys all named Robert
and after seventeen years
I began to forget which one of them I was

now whenever anyone gets uppity with me
and in return i puff up majestically to say

do you know who i am?
when they say
no
I get to say

neither do I
neither do I

FRIEND
(FOR GEORGE KERR)

somewhere between old yeller
and pythias you stand
firm in my closest friendship

the honesty comes from you in words
while i push mine out
with a typewriter
hardly daring to touch the keys

i see something of the earth in you
the hardy peasant
who does not dream of beanstalks
as he tills the drying soil
the calloused hand
which will not chafe
on fantasies

i am such a flightier crow than you
i ask to grow the dove's wings
as you shake your head
and look for another worm

our friendship is
that we know what friendship is
that we have looked for gods
but not in each other
that we have battered the idols
but not one another

A TALL MAN WALKING FAST

a tall man
  walking fast
  down Queen Street
called out —

              "HEY UGLY!"

and everybody
  turned around

TIME RELEASE POEMS
(slogans, sayings, corrections, koans and connections)

Don't blame the mirror
for your face
☻

No matter which way you turn
there's always something you're not facing
☻

Busy is the man with many hats
and nothing to put them on
☻

There is no neck
like the head itself
☻

Kneading bread broadens the mind
☻

To hide a pin prick in a sword thrust
☻

To read by the light of burning pianos
☻

That's like setting yourself on fire
in order to see in the dark
☻

You're just fishing for hooks
☻

You're just bum-fucking the ostriches
☻

Remember — fire hates its own light
☻

A night is only as dark
as the people in it
☻

Being mixed up
makes the cake

TO HIS 20TH CENTURY LOVER

ah when all the night-times meet
and the firefly novas burst
i'll love you dear till apocalypse
or for a week (whichever comes first)

LIKE TWO BRANCHES

like two branches
locked in skins of ice
my arms are made beautiful
with reaching for her
i want something impossible
entangled in them
and it becomes me

o she has breasts, world
small breasts
that tilt up
into something in me
that overflows

every day
by her laughter in the house
by her eyes seeing me
by her gentle hands upon my body
i am made more beautiful

and when she lies naked on the bed
there's not a field of wheat
or slender stem of anything
can rival
the slender golden way
i am
as i bend
to kiss her

WHAT DEW IS

the sea is an urge
she has
on nights too still
when days lie flat out
on her
like sheets of sweet and silent water

the sea is an urge
and mountains are her deep desires
cast out
rain is something
held beyond her
something that she arches up her body
like a bridge to meet
but does not meet

and in the morning
when the buds and roots
are moving in her
when her body trembles like a blade of grass
and dawn breaks
no thread of wanting in her

dew
is her cool way
of being
satisfied

POEM FOR URSULA IN NEW YORK

i will imagine that your mouth
now tastes of apples, Ursula
just by chance, in that you have just
bitten into one
i will imagine that you have left
your room immediately
determined to overcome
your fear of the streets
you are right in the centre of the city
and all the traffic of the world
is moving round you
i imagine you feel a little like
swirling your skirts
strolling in your outrageous way
down some street
and the wild energy climbs your body
like a crackling ecstatic light, it lifts your
breasts, flings your hair, stares
amazed into your eyes and coming finally
on your man, whatever man
(may he be gentle with you),
leaves him like a white moth
just brushed by a hint of colour
with that taste
that aroma of apples
lingering on his lips

POEM OF THE TWO TONGUES

Already in my bastardized, anglophone poetics
Apparently I've asked this comely Quebecois
Not to dribble on my leg

And she in similar poetic spontaneity
Speaks some magnificent French phrase
Which severely titillates me, but is translated, she tells me as
"Your love is like vomited wine."

Everything, obviously is not going well
Admittedly, romantics have lead me astray
I've heard in our union the clanging of the Canadas
And I'm trying too hard, so
Determined not to irritate
The situation further
I resort to simple high-school French
"Aaah la nuit descend dans mon âme," I say.
"Tu es ma lune, mes étoiles, mon uh . . . "
And there I'm forced to stop

I want to say "You are the first red tongue of morning
Licking back black curls in the thighs of the night,"
But alas, I've never been a cunning linguist
And such a phrase is quite beyond my capabilities
O, I might say "You're the crack of dawn"
But even here my tongue might lead me into error, and
Besides, why should I stoop
To such an old and worn
Cliché! —

As it was I just stood there
Foolishly stuttering
And, touched, I suppose

By my child-like confusion
She leant forward and kissed me
"Enfant," she said, "no more words. Oui?"
"Oui," I answered sheepishly

And though later that night I did
Have two tongues in my mouth
For a time
It wasn't until we came
To that region known by some as
Le petit mort
That I began to worry again
How we might be made
Better countrymen

MOMMIES

the prime minister has admitted
he needs his mommy
he is down on the floor of the house of commons
crying like a child
in agreement for once, the leader of the opposition
has likewise admitted
that he needs his mommy
and the two of them are hoping
with the mingling of their griefs
to heal the world

so now the streets are filled with people
who claim to need their mommies —
the flower lady needs her mommy
the fish man needs his mommy
the bus conductor needs his mommy
it seems like everyone
whether he had one
or not
needs his mommy

dejected
great breasts sagging
dry to their navels
all the mommies
are trying to hide
they are worn out with births
their faces made featureless
with so many rough kisses
their limbs are flat
their hands are empty
and their souls are tired
but it is too late for them

laws are being passed
the prime minister is unhappy
the leader of the opposition is unhappy
the flower lady, and the fish man
and the bus conductor are unhappy
"Let their daughters serve time for them
in factories and bars," they cry

meanwhile, rounding up suspects
the mounties go from door to door
with earnest looks and a mirror
saying
"Do you recognize this woman?"

INSOMNIA

It is the sound of mothers washing their children
that keeps me awake — the scratch of brooms across
so many floors
and sometimes I know that one hand
doesn't know what the other hand is doing
and the sound of them finding one another
the blind gallop of one towards the other
in an office handshake
deafens me
If they meet in the streets
if they fidget with coins
then I know I will be sleepless
that night

It used to be hunger that kept me awake
I used to fidget about the silence —
how it was sustained by so many gunmen
Then I met commerce and politics
I stood up in auditoriums and heard
the clapping together of many hands
It is the envelopes now that get to me
the secret licking late at night
the scratch of pens — of nails along a back

I used to be kept awake by anger
by the loud gabble of people lying to themselves
I used to be wide-eyed at the prospect of success
Now I can't sleep for the sound
of one hand washing the other

THE CHANGE

i keep sending off life
but my messengers are not arriving

the suicides
keep calling out for something
some blood-letting maybe
just let the soul out a little
at the wrists
at the wrists
twist the voice
from its dry rag
just one last time
in pain

o my fools
my children
are babbling in the darkness
crying
with small sawn voices
for something
they can't have
just let the light in
let the light in a little
at the wrists
at the wrists

and so now i'm changing
my symbols are moving
against my death
the bird emerges from its shell
half-formed
still raw and shocked
the mouth beats a desperate

wing of blood
against the heart
and whatever it is a horse
means to me
has begun to gallop

IF

if i could maim that part in me
which generates this need for you
believe me i would

if distances could cut the threads
which tie me to you
how quickly i would put a world
between us

if i could nullify the time
and wrench each memory and vision
of you from its painful place in mind
like some ecstatic madman
in the green grass
i would tear you loose

if by denying gods
i might deny this pain
you engender in me
trees would be uprooted in my fury
rivers halted, frozen at the source
the winds contained, contaminated
with your name

i hack these words from silences
my loudest songs cannot dispel

if i could strike the summer
from its place among the seasons
though i wreck the whirling of the world
to rid myself of memory
my love
i would

FRANKENSTEIN

The Secret needs
Of a thousand women
Formed him
He would be handsome, heroic,
Hung well, but gentle — gentle
My tender ones
As a child

His hair would be golden
He would have a voice
That bobs like a ball
In his throat
He would fuck intuitively
Divining with his held hand
Your deepest secret source
Of need
He would lay upon you like the leaves
Upon the water
Or ride you only
Where you wish

When he's yours
This Frankenstein of needs
You will all fuck him senseless
You will fuck him night and day
As though he were a peg
You cleansed yourselves upon
As though he were a stall
You came to
And shut the door to use
He will have a hand
Without a line
A face sideways

I think he will be
The perfect monster for you

IF I HAVE BECOME A PRISON

Someone free my green-eyed woman
If a bond she has made of my embrace
Someone free my green-eyed woman
Free her and all her ancient race

And if I have become a prison
Let me be broken and empty
But if I have become a mirror
Let her learn to see the truth in me

Someone free my green-eyed woman
From her pain and from her cruelty
Someone free my green-eyed woman
From her race and from her family

For if they have become a prison
Let them be broken and empty
But if they have become a mirror
Let them show a face forever free

And if I have become a prison
Let me be broken and empty
But if I have become a river
Let her learn to cure her thirst in me
Let her see right to the heart of me

If I Have Become A Prison

by Robert Priest

Some-one free my green eyed

wo - - man If a bond she has

made of my em - - brace

Someone free my green eyed wo - - - man

Free her and all her an - cient

race And if I have be - come a
if they have be - come a

pr - ison Let me be bro-ken and
pri - son Let them be bro-ken and

emp - ty But if I have be - come a
emp - ty But if they have be - come a

mir - - ror Let her learn to see the
mir - - ror Let them show a face for -

truth in me Some-one free my
e - ver free

REVOLUTIONS
(FOR GALILEO)

i am a tall white thing that birds fly out of
that is why you see me in the morning so open-mouthed and
foolish
the doctor said
"you are upside down
you have a large wounded thing in your mouth
i would advise you to cry"
but i said "no doctor
you are wrong
i am tremulous and exultant — a green strand
drawn from the throat of a flower
i am the magnet the wind arrives at finally
those are songs you see lodged in me
if i cry there will be no passion in it
i have tried again and again to throw off these robes of water
but wherever i have whirled them —
there the drunken — the inexhaustible flowers
have followed and come groping up to me
with praises
why should i cry?"
"you're upside down" he said
"no" i replied, and i began to revolve in the air
in front of him
"you think it must be somewhere near here
that the ground is
the suicides have told you
the rain and snow have told you
it's down below
somewhere under the houses
but they are wrong
and you are wrong
i am that dancing man
who kicks over the jug of the stars

those are my tracks across the moon

wherever i put my feet
that is where
the ground is

THE RE-ASSEMBLED ATOM

it was time
there was too much light in the world
there were not enough cities
they had to
they re-assembled the atom

its centre they found
spiralled in a woman's womb
boring like a worm for the ovaries
its planets, each one lodged
at the base of the spine
spun out at the necks
of presidents and kings
bullets found them all
divine bullets
in holy surgery
whales swam ashore in suicidal shoals
to deliver its energy
its leaves were fossil leaves
an old woman disgorged them in a purge
they had its tongue and its moon and its memory
but still half of it was lost
half of it was the man
and half the child
its blood lived in wells
deep beneath the earth
it was half money
half starved
it was time
they stitched it all together
they had to
they called it the frankenstein atom
and waited

FLAGS

I
all those stars, those stars
do you think they like that small crammed corner?
that stuffed rectangular galaxy
each one waiting to nova?
o those stars, those stars
do you think they are learning brotherhood there?
efficiently arranged
and fenced in
by the stripes, the stripes, the stripes

II
the flags have all been unravelled by the wind
and rewoven
now we have the stitched —
the united frankenstein flag —
the patchwork skin of countries and countries
or the blended — the flag deleted
X'd out by its own profusion
moon flag — memorial to wind
trapped undulation of imaginary airs

the face flag rippling
in a cheek
o the flags and flags of blood
flapping half-masted
for freedom
o still flag
inscrutable rag
of the sky

TARGET PRACTICE
(THE BULL'S EYE)

the bull's eye is the scapegoat
minus its face
stripped of its uniform and nationality
no religion or name
it is the narrow telescopic end
of the mirror
an accidental twin you can't help
killing again and again
immortal, eternal there in its circles
a bland enemy
you can never destroy

the bull's eye is the angel
you go hunting for
when winter comes yet again
it is a flock of fathers
finally made small
a round outlaw in hiding
zeroed in on
and paralysed

it is the last child
the last animal
the last great love

the bull's eye
is your anger compressed
made efficient and holy
ringed by a dozen haloes
it is the bright erupting dot
of a hatred
that practice only makes
more perfect

LESSER SHADOWS

the buildings wait for the assassins

the shadows are prepared for them —
they flow like dark sheets
of blood from underneath the doors

there are many vacant rooms
many rifles waiting

soon the assassins begin to arrive
they are all a little crazy
moved by politics or dark desires
they are tense and frightened
but eager, jostling one another
for places at the windows

there are assassins behind bushes
assassins on roofs
and distant hilltops
there are so many assassins
there are assassins crouched
in shadows of assassins

it is good that the victim is young
and wealthy
it is good that
he seems to symbolize something

now they prepare their weaponry
his car goes by
the triggers click
a thousand bullets meet
inside a single head

the skull explodes
the president is dead
silently
some with spittle running
from the corners of their mouths
some dazed
as though awaking from a trance
the assassins file out of the buildings
past the shocked, staring faces to the highways
past the farthest edges of the sun's descending red
and, as night absorbs the lesser shadows
America absorbs her murderers
completely

EXCUSES
(FOR ALLENDE)

There were too many amputated limbs
dancing in the streets
and i had to aid a man divided
by his own hands
suddenly the air was thick with flies
i would have heard the gunfire
but there was a parade of patriotic gates
and doorways in my street
and just then the shadow of a sparrow fell
it fell for hours
blotting out everything
if you had cried louder
there would have been thunder i'm sure
a dispute about mining rights

i would have heard the gunfire
i might have seen him fall
but i was on the wrong side
of too many borderlines
i would have heard the earth cracking
i would have heard the first
of the excuses

ARE THERE CHILDREN

are there children somewhere
waiting for wounds
eager for the hiss of napalm
in their flesh —
the mutilating thump of shrapnel
do they long for amputation
and disfigurement
incinerate themselves in ovens
eagerly
are there some who try to sense
the focal points of bullets
or who sprawl on bomb grids
hopefully
do they still line up in queues
for noble deaths

i must ask:
are soul and flesh uneasy fusions
    longing for the cut —
    the bloody leap to ether
are all our words a shibboleth for silence —
a static crackle
to ignite the blood
and detonate the self-corroding
    heart
does each man in his own way
plot a pogrom for the species
or are we all, always misled
to war

Glasnost

Glasnost

Glaszjnoss

glassnnoss

glazznish

glassness

glawzniss

klashness

klowzniss

klowsnis

kloshness

klostness

closdness

closedness

DEC. 8, 1980

I think John Lennon is falling
He takes two steps, two more steps
and a hole opens in the earth
five holes in the earth
and John Lennon is falling
Falling from my childhood
Falling from the earth
Two steps he takes
Two more steps
and then he falls face forward
We can't believe it
He falls through our arms
through our tears
We might be ghosts for all we can do
to stop him
He falls from a thousand buildings
in a huge rain of bodies
They are shooting him out of the skies
shooting him in San Salvador
shooting him in Santiago
Lennon's blood flows into the Hudson
It flows down the Mississippi
A red tide reaches Britain's shores
His blood soaks into the setting sun
He stains the Japanese coast
John Lennon is falling out of the sky
saying one last thing to us

his eyes wide
his lips moving
saying one last thing
we can't quite hear
It is too sudden

The earth opens
There is a hole in the sky
five holes in heaven
and Lennon is falling out of sight
into the sky
smashing into the earth
first one foot
then the other foot
just two steps
just two more steps
and then he falls face forward
into our arms
deep into the world
Lennon falls

DISGUISES

there is a saying among pigs
"Be a pig to the very end"
but sometimes just outside the abattoirs
you will see one of them break down
and start to wear a hat
others you might see dressed in habits
trying to sneak into church with the nuns
and it is not just the pigs
who have taken to wearing disguises
for who has not heard the tale
of those sheep
who wore grey suits and tried to enter
with the businessmen
who has not caught lately
a catfish in a cap
or a turkey
in a punk suit

in times such as these
we must observe our fellows closely
always ask as the butcher slits another throat
"Now who is putting on
a red tie?"

CONCERNING MY OBSESSION WITH BLOOD

if i bite into an apple
and the apple breaks in blood
if i wake up and it is raining blood
if lunatics dance joyously
open-mouthed in blood
if all the palaces and stock exchanges
temple walls and factories shall
reek of blood
if blood shall rot in gutters
flood the streets
and stain the mountain peaks
and valleys
in its unceasing red monsoon
if blood shall seep up through the soil
and mat the grass
if flags are stiff and clotted
to the staff with blood
if khans and kings
their emperors and generals
and savage soldiers
shall be glutted, stuffed
and sick with blood

then i will write a poem
about water

A POEM ABOUT WATER

water is something
i want to make perfectly clear
i want to come clean about water
i'm saying the water is dirty
the holy water
in our hearts and mouths and bellies
water is a gem
we come shivering out of
it is the earth
toiling at the earth
a silver mistress
who lulls with singing
the giant reach of land
to stony slumber
water is the earth
reflecting on itself
a liquid contemplation
of the moon and sun
of the distant stars and abysses
that people looking down
might see the beginning
and the end
of thirst

VANCOUVER FROM MOUNT SEYMOUR

Water worshipers
This is your church
Where all the fallen footsteps
Lurch like drunken Giants
To their final frozen prayer
This is your mountain altar
In the still cathedral air

Secret sinners
This is your tabernac
Upon this broken bristle
Of the wild hogs back
The fleas shall sing and whistle
To a final frenzied bow
This is the butchered udder
Of your former sacred cow

Speed and acid trippers
This is your hit
Where all the punctured junkies
Slit like Jack-o-lanterns
In their final fractured mirth
Ride the milk-white moon cows
As they jump the sleeping earth

POEM FOR THE ANCIENT TREES

I am young and
want to live
to be old
and I don't want to
outlive these trees —
this forest
when my last song is gone
I want these same trees
to be singing on —
newer green songs
for generations to come
so let me be old
let me grow to be ancient
to come as an elder
before these same temple-green sentinels
with my aged limbs
and still know a wonder that will outlast
me
O I want long love
long life
give me 150 years
of good luck
but don't let me outlive these trees

MONEY

All the dirt on money clean off onto your headstone
and coins with faces worn down by a million palms
nothing on it but the polyglot fingerprint
the big thumb of nerves beneath which we all cower

All the dirt on money clean off into a lake
the great glacial eye rotating on its skein of sights
uncovers quicksilver creeping in the hatchery
the death rattle of Iroquois and salmon

All the filth and nervousness of money
contracted in a handshake
the great golden jingle that sucks out the water
and dirties it
little mirrors jingling with my king-face
and beasts extinct

All the breath breathed in want of money
all the deeds done for money
this round catalogue of agonies and consumption
this devouring head
o amulets ceaselessly fingered
o economy

QUICKSILVER *

There are those who say there's nothing you possess
Beyond your soul in pain or happiness
But there are others with their marks upon the soil
Who live to bend their brothers' backs in toil

Our fathers came here for their liberty
But where they wandered only blood ran free
From the silver lake to the broad prairie
Now the rivers run with mercury

And our blood is sick with mercury
And the tears fall like mercury
Life slips away like mercury
And we get quicksilver, quicksilver quicksilver
For all your cold gold

Somehow the native people have survived
Four hundred years of outright genocide
To hear the English and the French sing a sad sad song
All about how they did each other wrong

With a voice torn from soil and torn from stone
I say again there's nothing you can own
And you better watch just what you do
Cause all your deeds come back on you

Then your money melts like mercury
And your tears fall like mercury
You life slip away like mercury
And you get quicksilver quicksilver quicksilver
For all your cold gold

*Notation for this song can be found at www.poempainter.com

TIME RELEASE POEMS

One wind moves many flags
❀
Daylight respects no borders
❀
O Canada our
stolen native land
❀
Nous peuvent seulement separer ensemble
❀
U.S. is not us
❀
Every little ruler wants a 13th inch
❀
Be bold
or be bowled over
❀
True marksmen see beyond guns
❀
Hurrying to meet the panther
❀
Never doubt the tiger's sincerity
❀
A clam is only as big
As its own mouth
❀
No one can see the whole cloud
❀
To be "between lovers"
at the moment
❀
To mop yourself out of the room
❀

Practical is ruthless
with gloves on

❂

There is nothing so efficient
as the last match

❂

To be "between enemies"
at the moment

❂

You cannot kiss ass and kick it too

❂

The most dangerous people are the obedient

❂

Quislings with no Reich

MEDIUM

just a hole
a portal
one rib in a long transit
just a part where
something goes through
its purpose to permit transgression
to be at once entrance exit
mouth and throat
small skin puncture
in the inner arm

the stomach
never to remain full
always peristalsis
the downward spirals
of digestion
to a point
out
of you

all this highway
that i am
a gulp at something
always going through me

neither the beginning
nor the end
of a swallow

THE DOOR KNOB

the door knob teaches centuries
of hands
the art of revolution
we thought of it twisting
off the heads of kings
and when the flowers came up uncurling
as though from circles underground
we thought of it again

the holy door knob
teaches us the art of entry —
rotate the wrist
and great worlds will come
spinning out of it
turn that small knob of brass
and the whole mountain will unravel
like the twisting of a thousand
snakes

ODE TO THE CLITORIS

little bud
of nerves
all other limbs
are slaves
to your standing up —
vassals to uplift you
in a holy arch of ivory
you are a point in radar
pulsing out
your sonic bleep
to all extremities
where else in nature
shall i find your like
if not strung out
green and undulating
from some river-splitting
rock
you are the water dropped
a thousand miles
into a wide disjointed
ocean
dawn's first red tongue
of light
lapping at the wide-spread night
you are the hub
of the body —
the tender, topmost
leaf
of the ecstatic tree
you are a box
of sweet lightning
someone breaks open
with a kiss

POST-MODERN PENIS

in its cowl
like a monk
its head hung over
in humility

like a bloodhound
half up
out of the docket
nose high
with the first thick scent
of some right woman

neglected, hung up
like your mother's old coat
on a hook
for a month
unwashed
the stains still on it

another mind
supernaturally smart
another
wrinkled heart

half-hard
arched down the eye slit
just leering out
from it prepuce patch
up periscope

the bathing penis
high in its crow's nest
buffoon-like

twirled clown
stupid root pig bit
stunted arm blood balloon
testicle companion
testicle exclamation
sinking in bit
delivering bit
with its backbone up
with its fine etched veins
pulsing visible in sex juice
this divining bone
manpart, heartroot
this hung cheese
this hung hog
in a butcher's shop
this disobedient flaccid dog
in its too-big suit
in its wrinkled robes
old patriarch
flung down
by god
sacred king
hanged man
tiddlybit
pee pee

tiniest tube
in the big
bone
world

ODE TO THE BUM

due to my profound
knowledge
of the human soul
i can no longer see
even the most shapely
of bums
as anything
but a manifestation
of
duplicity

CHERRIES

O cherries
what could be rounder
or more regal than you?
hanging in your kingdoms there
so royal and red
I love you to your pits
you meaty kings
you unexploded suns
waiting for the ignition
of another mouth
look!
I turn a key into your
rotundity
and several laughing buddhas
spring out tickled
it has been a long age
cherry
that we have danced beneath
your bulging boughs
not daring to change the symmetry
of a single royal cluster
but now there is a revolution
in the hands
a usurper we protected
in astrologies of seed
uncurls inside you

So then my mirthful
perfect kings
my many times duplicated kings
come to me by ones
and by twos
and I will show you

the kingdom in my belly
where you at last may end
your perfect journeys
down from godhead
to be in my
red blood

THE ASSHOLE

exclamation dot
dropped off at the bottom of you
an apertured lens
visible only in slang moments
a hairy star

the finest
circle of instinct ever
elastic sensate
highly responsive
it holds us in and issues us
joins the inner and outer worlds
the true halo
organic wedding band
most of all it's home
to instinct, evolution
a kind of water well
from which all rings
move outward
up through shores
of grief and bone
to brow and brain

it lets wisdom in
and hot air out

but not too proud
nor too vulnerable
for the darkest possible tasks
this snake of devolution and decay
this period at the end of you
bottom crown
blow hole

starlip

radar and trumpet
this peaceful
thoughtful
anus

TIME RELEASE POEMS

A soul/asshole
>
The other end of the rose
>
The observer *is* the event
>
You're not truly naked till you bend over
>
The proctologist's eyebrow
>
Trust your lust
>
Safety 5th
>
If the sickness don't get you the cure will
>
If the famine don't get you the feast will
>
If the thirst don't get you the water will
>
If the celibacy don't get you —
>
To fall in love (with a parachute)
>
To drown in the surface tension
>
To search for the needle of disappointment
In the haystack of your blessings
>
To love more
And fear less
>
A flower cannot keep
From the sun

❖
Iron blames the magnet

❖
Good lovers come in pairs

I KNEW I COULD SING (INDUSTRIAL ACCIDENT NO. 1)

I knew I could sing
when my hand got sucked into the rollers at the factory
cause I hit a high note then that they said
was heard over the sound of the machines
all the way up to the front office

Even as the rollers whirred and burned
and gnawed at my flesh
my mind in its detached way
was listening to that note
marvelling at its purity

I was deep in shock
by the time the men ran over
and finally turned the machine off
The great cylinder ground to a stop
and just weighed down there —
a painful rim
like a whole world
squashing my hand

When they finally unscrewed the housing
(there was no safety release at all)
it took three men to lift up
the great fallen log of the roller
and then as the blood rushed back in
to the white branch of my hand
I knew I could sing
I knew I could sing

WHY I CRUSHED MY HAND

I crushed it for my girlfriend
I crushed it for my dad
I crushed it for my mom and my squashed history
in the head
I crushed it for factory safety —
a young martyr at sixteen
I crushed my hand because I wanted to see what it was like
for the school system and workmen's compensation
just to have a story
because there was a piece of paper caught in the roller
and I wanted to get it out
so I grabbed at it and got sucked in
feeling a great tug on the flesh
all the way up my arm
I crushed my hand for world peace because I wanted to stop
the fighting in viet nam
no — I wanted to get out of my homework
I wanted people to stop hitting me
and I wanted a kiss from those
Indian lips of hers
those dark kisses
of Shamim*

I crushed my hand because I hated working in the factory
I wanted to be out in the sun and I wasn't having this
60 dollars a week
40 dollars a week is what I got on compensation
and this skin graft on my hand
where the flesh was burned off in an oval egg shape

I crushed my hand because I wanted to get the paper out of the rollers
because I had heard the story over the supper table
a million times before

because I wanted to know the careless violence of machines —
metal without pity, just power surging —
to sing, to do a great circus act, a man with a hand like a white leaf
WHOOP, a man with a hand like steak
a purple football, a man with a hand like a great yellowing yam
big as hell in the bed, in the cast
I crushed my hand to give starving doctors work
to keep the hospital going
because I wanted to see what plastic surgery was like
I was young and I wanted to meet a physiotherapist
I had never had manual whirlpool baths before
and my guts, my guts were ready because it was the damn hand
that picked up the phone, that got the news, that got the refusal
the rejection, blackened by plastic over the wires —
a baleful voice saying no saying no

because it had dared wave goodbye
because it had been in the service of the empire and was tainted
and needed to be punished
now I wouldn't have to do my share of the housework
I could just walk around with that large bandage
the hand held high, in traction
as though in greeting and look like a holy man or a fool
I crushed my hand to find the hidden map in the flesh
that would lead me to poetry, to you and to the page
I crushed it to get out of there and get my ticket stamped
and get on with it

*my first girlfriend (a native of South Africa) who had recently rejected me.

INDUSTRIAL ACCIDENT NO. 2

One minute the fingers were quite straight
and beautiful
I was pushing a plank lengthwise
into a table saw and I said to myself —
"Be careful now — your hand is getting close to the blade
and you've already had one accident."
Then the buzz saw bit into me
with a singing twang
splattering blood over three walls
in a wide halo of drops

My hand seemed to be ringing
like a bell as
I held it up in horror —
all the fingers exploded outward
like red flowers at the tips
My other hand grasped
tourniquet-tight about the wrist
"Take me to the hospital" I screamed
jumping up and down

Now one finger is permanently bent and stiff
On cold days I don't dare type with it
and it is useless for picking up dimes
Nor is it good for pointing out directions or fault
knowing as I do
that finger is always somewhat
pointing back at me

POETRY IS . . .

there are those who lay bricks
there are those who break rocks with picks
there are those who work on assembly belts
there are those who care for children
there are sex workers
and there are those who make poems

turn on the belt and begin
the great clacking of the typewriter
smashing at the rock in the paper
thumping at the door in the paper
pushing at the bird in the paper
shaping and re-shaping the poem
holding it up to the light

there is the carpenter
and then further along down the river is the poet
filling up, systematically
the clean white rectangle
clang clang clang
his silver hammer arcs high in the sun
as he cracks through the mica surface
jang jang jang
as he shatters the diamonds there
looking for bright
truths

poetry is
manual labour

MY GRANDFATHER LIVES

my grandfather lives
in the bluest skies ever
too late for my goodbye kiss
gone now that i have never embraced him
gone —
but young again in memory
returned
to his blessed carpentry

goodbye grandfather
my arms never once went round you
and it is too late now

you have left us
only each other
to embrace

THE HAMMER

the blind hammer
beats its eye
upon the nail

sight won't break
open in it

can't even see
inside itself

but is just darkness
and a voice that holds
the houses up

PRIDE

i have a window on myself
and watch in solitude
the moon rising up out of me

i am a slender poet
and all my limbs, especially my fingers
are roots
the earth i find myself in nurtures little
in me
i look inside and see
my hands stretched
into the darkness, out of their element
with reaching after needs
but a tree stands upon my solitude
each bud of it an imploded leaf
i couldn't bear the beauty of
that hard nut — pride
is absorbing the oak
my veins my arteries reach
for some word i might speak
but no — the shrinking —
the withering from myself
continues

and so inside
i keep my hatred
hoping it will not find
fertility
it is cold — an artery
of frost that fires conduct
breath through —
see, my lips have become a sneer
my arms are empty

boughs that bend
to no longing
this year is my ache
and the ache of my ancestors
suddenly pushed onto me
so i fold into my sterile centre like a seed that won't grow

but a tree stands upon my solitude
and it can't twist its awful sinews
to look back
my arms are disappearing
my mouth is disappearing
all my black oaken limbs are disappearing
and a forgotten child —
a child i cannot bear the beauty of
is falling into my arms

MY FATHER'S HANDS

My father had so many hands
He had almost three
My father had so many hands
He had almost three
My father had almost three hands
But not enough
To touch me once gently

O my father had so many eyes
He had almost three
My father had so many eyes
He had almost three
My father had almost three eyes
But not enough to see me
Once perfectly

My father had but one mouth
And one heart
To lift those bales and bales
At the factory
My poor father of fists and fists
Beating at the wall
Beating at his brow
Beating at his children

My poor factory father
Lined and fat-bellied now
Tranquillized and happier
Made smaller by so many sons
The winds gave him only one
Heart
And they said
"Here — spin it

Make it the hole in rock
We whistle shrill through
Grit your teeth and count your children"

He wonders what to do with
Hands now
Where to put them —
These tender lined things
That ache for sons
O my father we are here —
The prints of wanting
Emblazoned on us like
Radioactive brands

My father had so many hands
And he waves them now —
Ashamed a little
Looking puzzled as we leave
At the movement from his wrist
As if he wondered — what are they
When they are not fists

MY MOTHER'S HANDS

They call me over the wilderness
over the waves, fingers in dials
fingers in rings, through keyboards of ivory
wringing themselves
bone dry
they call
that sewed with thimbles
those raw things, those dangerous hands
poet's, painter's hands, trapped in a woman
hands of mind, dripping with talent always talking
of slitting themselves open at the wrist
and just running away from it all
saying "sometimes I just feel like dying —"

In certain shapes memories are kept
flashing for a moment over the ages
as though from a genetic shore —
warnings, beauties, secrets
mother, mother —
this poem should be about your blood
your blood in the bath
threatening to be there
diluting the water behind the locked door
where you washed yourself making no sounds
"Mom"
as we lay awake in the room beside you
in our beds, calling out at regular intervals
"Mom"
just to make sure the life hadn't just slid out of you in there
in a slow freezing rush

Mother
this poem should be about the white of statues

the way you would say "this time I'm not coming back"
and walk away after arguments or blows
wrath, down the street
a long way to where it bends
and then turn
me praying, giving up preposterous rights
anything to god to jesus
to whatever it was that had the power to reassure me

Eventually she always came back
her hands freezing in the coat
having walked it off I suppose
cooled out
back
with a kiss
to show us
that brutality
can have the softest face
the most gentle hands
of all

NOW THERE IS RAIN

Where your eyes were now there is rain
and where your lips were now there is anguish
O where the touching was
now, Rafiki, now there is pain
your absence so awesome to us
we ache outside it
like children in a winter

O what a long cold wind your death sends
whistling through us
What a galaxy of tears — tears that shine
with your grace remembered

Where your brown skin was
now the leaves drift past
It is one of those days
always one of those days when pain gnaws in the air
pain in the brittle grass
and the distant cruel sun

Ah Rafiki my sweet babe
no more can I cup my hands
into the water of your life and see myself
gleeful in your love
no more the rain of your life upon my life
so bright, so bright in the days
You are gone in the river of light, my child
over smooth lands to the sea you go
dissolved in the sun at the edge of the world

Your soul in its star — distant and beautiful
cut from us in time
in your little boat

Wait for us my child
beyond the reefs of eternity

for Rafiki Cruise April 1, 1978 — October 28, 1981

MY INFECTED RAINBOW

i took my infected rainbow to the rainbow-doctor
totally white sam
and he said what's wrong with it
so i said well just feel it, it's all misty
and it can't even arch over anything
it just dwindles smaller and smaller each day
leaving little stains in the sky
i can't erase
Perhaps it needs a transfusion he said
have you bled into it lately
no i said it's just not sharp enough
any more so he took some of my yellow blood
and he injected it into the top of the rainbow
and some of my black for the bottom
and slowly i watched the seep of the colour through it
the reinvigorated, the refreshed rainbow
flowing in sediments to its
true brilliance
then when it shone like neon
the doctor darkened his office
and we with our faces lit up
knelt down upon our knees
and so made something
for it to arch over

there he whispered to me
now all you need is a wind surgeon
and a healer of leaves . . .

O no! i shouted, look —
the colour's running out again
look at the apples!
look at the butterflies!

so he examined the rainbow's wrists
and said
you don't need me
you need rasputin
this rainbow's
a haemophiliac!

TIME RELEASE POEMS
(or: more slogans, sayings, corrections, koans and connections)

Whitewash comes in many colours

✵

There is no peace for the punching bag

✵

Too much time is wasted in the making of clocks

✵

There is no camouflage like a good philosophy

✵

Cars — people fleeing in their problems

✵

Clothes make the man — poor

✵

Forgive and remember

✵

Never say "Never say never"

✵

When you deny you deny you deny!

✵

You can't go down from the bottom

✵

There is no trampoline like the bottom of the soul

✵

The edge comes from within

✵

Do you travel for the journey
or just for the arrival?

✵

Different destinations
but for a while the same path

✵

You can't murder the dead

✵

You can't forgive yourself
without forgiving others

❀

A sweet tongue won't cure a rotten tooth

❀

There is nothing worse for men than overcoming giants

❀

To blow out the match and the candle too

❀

Don't call your own shadow the night

❀

Don't love the rose only for its thorns

❀

Don't sharpen the arrow as it hits you

❀

Don't bother climbing up a falling man

❀

When the last light goes out
what is the speed of darkness?

WHAT KIND OF VOODOO

I throw darts at dots in a circle on the wall
If i puncture the little spot in the middle of the dot
Of red paint I feel free

What kind of Voodoo do you do
What kind of Voodoo do you do

I put antlers on my head and joined the lodge
I spoke the ancient vows and didn't dodge
The drop of paint they spattered on my tongue
It made me feel so young

What kind of Voodoo do you do
What kind of Voodoo do you do

I just put on the gloves and pull out the bag
And smack the sucker silly then I wave the flag
And feel so absolutely free
They put a medal on me

What kind of Voodoo do you do
What kind of Voodoo do you do to who

No its not the same o don't you see
There's no similarity
'Cause we're the guardians of
Civilization

I attend a local place where songs are sung
And they put a little kind of wafer on my tongue
Then we drink the blood of jesus christ
Really its juice — it tastes quite nice

What kind of Voodoo do you do
What kind of Voodoo do you do

WHEN MY FAITH LEAPS

when my faith leaps
like a man who has a bird
and lets it go
i leap after it

it keeps bringing me
twigs and things
to build temples on

at first i trusted it
but since the house of Christ
fell down on me
and the house of the cry ate at me
and since lately it's been
bringing me things like
arms, like a heart
and a ghost
and since it just brought me
a face
strangely familiar

when my faith leaps
like a man with a short memory
and an exceedingly long tale
i leap after it

GHOST REMOVAL*

Getting out a burnt stoat ghost is hard
First you must dig a hole and spit in it
then run at the hole as though
you were going to dive in but instead
suddenly stop
A true stoat ghost will be unable
to resist continuing into the hole

Falling will release bird ghosts
(which is my problem — everyday my breast is full
of a thousand ghostly wings but I am afraid to fall)

You must keep company constantly with a rodent
to rid yourself of eagle ghosts —
no amount of burning roses
will do

To remove the ghost of a slave takes high trickery
You must wait on top of a mountain until a royal procession
is in sight and then run down bowing and making
obsequious loyalist statements. A true slave ghost
will never be able to resist waiting on the peak and laughing
hoping to see his former master go by

Rat ghosts are hardest of all to remove
for you must go down with the rats into the sewers
You must wait with them there all summer
raving as rats rave
Then, when Autumn comes and they begin to chant
you must remain silent
That is when the rat will abandon your body
for a true rat
can never resist chanting, all through Autumn

deep underground
when the first of the leaves begin to fall

*Of late there are increasing reports of stray ghosts taking up
habitation uninvited in people's bodies. This poem is intended as
a guide to the removal of some of the more common varieties.

HOW TO PRAY TO A WOMAN

First you have to find the right woman —
You have to go into the streets and out to parties.
You have to look through magazines and watch the television —
Lose yourself entirely in the search for the right woman
each face you see like a leaf in a stream
carrying you off further and further into the space you must
occupy.

When you find the right woman
unfortunately you have to be indirect.
For, as you know, it is illegal to pray directly to a woman
in most countries of the world.
But, if it is a one time thing, sometimes you can just kneel
casually, and as though suddenly clapping the tiny body
of a mite somewhere about her ankles
utter while this delusion lasts
a few well chosen words such as
"Oh please! Oh please!"
If the woman says "What?"
you will have to cover up.
"Oh just saying fleas."
"Just a joke." You must cover up quickly
for if she suspects you have slipped a prayer on her
she can legally say "Look pal, I'm not your mother, you know!"

To practise praying to a woman, it can be helpful
to set up a mop, a broom or a welcome mat
and beg most intensely for her return.
When she comes in at last you must squat secretly in the closet
and as she chooses her dress for work unleash all the passion
of your religious convictions.
Try to hide the whisper of your prayer in the sound of her
nylons

rubbing together.
"Oh please, dear woman, help us clean up the cities. Oh please
let there be unity in our cradles."
If you can succeed in going to bed with a woman
you actually have a perfect chance to trick her into being
prayed to for quite a while.
Just tell her you would like it if she stood up
while you gave her head.
Then as you lick away you can pray, pray for eternal life
for the whole long list of everything —
Divine offspring and the new world.
You can pray until she comes
remembering to say "a-woman" gratefully as she bends and groans
finally to grant the first and most difficult part
of your wish.

HOW TO PRAY TO A TOILET

To pray to a toilet is very easy
if you are literate
Simply write your prayer down
on a piece of paper
and place it in the water
at the bottom of the toilet
Say
"Our toilet"
and flush

SEVERAL OTHER USES FOR A HALO

use it as the brim of a hat
the rim of a little wheel
put it for support in a pipe-line
up your arm and over your shoulder
reach through a halo and try
to get a hold of something in heaven
a halo is a kind of condom over your hand then
a sacrament of hygiene
a kind of navel in the sky
where you were cut
from umbilical sun-strings

dance in a hat made of the halo
shit through the halo
put your dick through the halo and pee
bounce the halo on pavement
put your halo in the hand of a friend
and entrust it there
like your own genitals
only exceedingly more tender
more sensitive
there are nerves in a halo more delicate
than diamonds
nerves that turn and receive
sending in messages and meaning
to your sensorium
put your halo back up in the sky
and look through it —
play the halo on your turntable
tie it to a dog, to a pig, to an elk, to a bison
let wild animals drag the halo off
drop the halo out of jet planes
put the halo in barbed wire

put it round a starved man
let it hover over a child
reach for your better self
through the hole in the halo
give the halo to your enemy
entrust the halo to random burials

let the halo be heaved from mound to mound in ghostly
quoits
do gymnastics on the halo, swing from the halo
find the high arc of heaven as you let the halo go
sell the halo
melt it down and pass it round
put the halo in boxes
hammer out the haloes
long thin wire of the haloes
bury the haloes beneath the earth
mountains of haloes
mould the haloes in mammon faces
send the haloes skipping over water
gold teeth of the haloes
jewellery of the haloes

you don't need the halo any more
you are ready to let the halo go
you have to put the halo on a hook
you have to put the halo on a hook
and just walk away from it

II
If you set up a halo in a winter sky
then, when the coldest winds howl through it
they activate old voices in misery
voices out of Hell on earth
The cries snuffed out by rifles and machetes
the cries snuffed out by grave dirt

Haloes can unleash these horrors which
are ravelled into the air
listen in the winter wind and see if you
detect the presence of fallen haloes
the pressure of punctures, bone-rimmed holes
where torment finds its stiff round mouth at last
o blow the bugles of bone
o beat the drums of bone
let the slaughtered dead arise again in song
listen
listen my christian ones
to the howling of the wind

CHRIST IS THE KIND OF GUY

Christ is the kind of guy
you just can't help hurting
No matter how much you love him
when you walk you stumble into him
you push him accidentally from a window
If you back the car out
you will find him squashed behind the wheels
broken on the door — all over the grate
Christ has the kind of skin
that bruises when you hold him
the kind of face that
kisses cut
He is always breaking open
when we go to embrace him
Christ the haemophiliac
even the gentlest people can't help
wounding Jesus Christ
They are always running for a band-aid
and then pulling open his old wounds
on a nail
If there is a cross in your house
you will find yourself bumping up against him
accidentally
moving him closer and closer to it
his arms continually more and more
widespread as he talks
Christ is the kind of guy
who can't help falling asleep like that
his arms spread wide as though over the whole world
You have a dream with a hammer
You are making a house
In the morning you awake
and find him up there on the crossbeams

one hand nailed to the door frame
"Look Jesus" you say
"I don't want to be saved like this!"
But then you hurt him
extra
taking him down
you pry at the nails savagely
but it's no use
Christ is the kind of saviour
you can only get off a cross
with a blow torch
"Father forgive them" he says
as you begin to burn his hands

GETTING CLOSE TO GOD

Perhaps you want to know
the agony of the starved
the horrible ecstasy of those
closest to god

Perhaps you want to get as close to god
as the child in the jungle
the child with the belly bloated
like a Buddha

Perhaps you want to be blasted to bits
baked in a bomb blast
You can almost see god's eyes then
a kind of grace enters you
a temporary ecstasy

We must examine god
in all the positions
We have to know which way to point
where to pray to —
Do you ever find him in the eyes
of dying soldiers?
on both sides, behind the rocket launchers
the ancient carbines
crouching in the dark
the little scared glints
in eyes?

Perhaps we must get close to the people
to get close to god
We must take them in our arms
and then Judah is in our arms
and Krishna is in our arms

We must make of each victim
a passageway to divinity
We must go amongst the poor
and feed god in them
We must fatten god up in the poor

Perhaps god is starving
in us

TESTAMENT OF A NEW FAITH

as soon as you give birth to a faith
you must begin to heap scorn on it
defile and despise your faith
heap all the world's filth on it
fill it up with stains from the worst acts
of mankind
degrade and abuse your temple
make it the slaughterhouse, the hospital
put your faith through the morgue
let your faith house even the murdered dead
and when you come at last to tear it down
for a failure

if it still stands
if the stone is white underneath
if you wash it off
and it still shines in the sun
with an untempered divinity
then you have a Faith
such as I have

CHRIST AFTER CHRIST

The shadow in the cradle draws a line across your life
Divided by each dawn that slips a day in like a knife
The long unending cry of the child denied unfolds
In the hangman, who's he hanging from his gallows of gold

But Christ after Christ after Christ after Christ
How many more must we sacrifice

Whales swim ashore in suicidal shoals
All just to see the second coming
Soldier going mad his eyes as bright as coals
Is it your blood or his blood or my blood that's running

From Christ after Christ after Christ after Christ
They're all lined up for paradise
How many more must we sacrifice

Seed-mouth deep in the soil won't break
Starved man sittin' with his emptiness and ache
Till the star-sea moves in the night's last bed
Hunger will walk wherever it is lead

By Christ after Christ after Christ after Christ
They're all lined up for paradise
How many more must we sacrifice

Christ After Christ

by Robert Priest

The shad-ow in the crad-le draws a line ac-ross your life Di-

vid-ed by each dawn that slips a day in like a knife The long un-end-ing cry of the

child de-nied un-folds In the hang-man, who's he hang-ing from his gal-lows of gold B-

chorus

Christ af-ter Christ af-ter Christ aft-er Christ

How man-y more must we sac-ri-fice

Whales swim a-shore in su-i-ci-dal shoals All just to see the se-cond com-ing

Sol-dier go-ing mad his eyes as bright as coals Is it your blood or his blood or

my blood that is run-ning But The seed-mouth deep in th

soil won't break   Starved man sit - ting with his emp - ti - ness and ache

Till the star - sea moves   in the night's last bed   Hun-ger will walk

Hun - ger will walk   Hun - ger willwalk where e - ver it is lead by

Christ af - ter Christ   af - ter Christ   aft - er Christ

How man - y more   must we sac - ri - fice

TIME RELEASE POEMS

Having subdued nature man now wishes to subdue the divine
❀
Thank god for the devil
❀
Music is the devil's agony
❀
A curse is a prayer
to the devil
❀
To fall in hate
❀
To parachute from grace
❀
Love ruins devils
❀
The quick leaping quantum Gods
in their Olympus of foam
❀
In my father's house are many Mansons
❀
Turn the other cheek
or I'll turn it for you
❀
To kiss it worse
❀
To have partial omniscience
❀
Yahweh or Noweh at all
❀
One thing in a row
❀
Wind to the hate mills
Wind to the hate mills

COME TO ME

come to me
I know we are out of sync
I know they will call it dying
but come to me anyway
I have tried to hate you with the strength
of many animals and I cannot hate you
so come to me burning
and I also will burn
come to me with ancient music and I will be a snake
writhing with my many wrists
each one more undulant than your long hair
o I still have nights and nights of you
all queued up in the thirst of a single slave
to work out
come to me with snow and I will promise
to be red in it
come to me unique and I will match you
stare for stare
come to me in greek in spanish in french in hebrew
and I will sing that I found you
because I overthrew reason
because I live in the wreck of my senses
by wish and magic
like a roc in the ruins of its egg
come to me dancing
that dark bacchanal of your kiss
so wet on my lips for days I will not want
drugs or water
just your own sea broken like a sheet of lightning
on your thigh so sensual
come to me because we will arrive
anyway at each other
because it has been many lives

and each time we touch
great forces
are again able to move
come to me cruel and lovely
because I am abandon
because I am silver
because a million years
you have suffered in slavery to men
and know at last how to be free

THE LONGER BED

for you, tall woman
the longer bed —
the bed stretched for sex
from hope to hope
sigh to sigh
each thigh prehistoric, immense
laid down on the road to the mouth
for you the catch undone
the bird gone soaring

and so i will get to you my love
and touch you so gently you will think
the wind has grown amorous animal hands
and so I will wander in the forces of your love
like a lost thing
searching for the centre —
the middle of the maelstrom
where i can calmly touch you and be burned —
charred at the mouth at the very base
of my blood
sizzled with a hot corrosive kiss —
one that welds me to you
melts my mouth to yours
for days tasting each other
far away

for you tall woman
a night to risk it all in
a night stretched for sex
taut against the meeting of our mouths
thigh to thigh
dawn to dawn
for you a longer bed

a bed to last and last
a bed you can only get into
over your head

THE CLOCK HAS GONE MAD

lie down love
the clock has gone mad
we are not living that fast
we need time
for each moment to sink in
to be felt
lie down and ignore the gibberish —
the zooming past of cars
ignore that clock
whirling like a roman candle
and look at this durable dark —
this dark that spreads from rim to rim
encompassing the world
it does not live so fast
it does not come
and then go like that
propelled out of existence
by the whirling hand of a machine
examine the depth of this night
which we plunge to the bottom of
with our deep kisses
see how it stretches the world over
and cannot be ended
by bomb blast or candle
love
we cannot rush this
undress slowly
let us love slow and long
feeling everything
let the knife slide in the butter
let the honey drip
from the spoon —

we will not be
that fast

WEDDING POEM

Come, let us be joined in holy coitus
Here by this wave lapping in
Here by this rock
I swear by our love that we are heaven's dynamo
Two industrial strength people
Spelling out our alphabet to industry and love
Yay and I do part your petals with this simple piston
And we do bang together
Letting up great hosannas of our most religious
And saved up exaltations
Yay yay my love and my rod is hard within you
Right in the clench of the divine
We are two rocks on a string
Two wings of an angel
Our bodies when they meet are like two hands
Praying

POEM FOR A TALL WOMAN

If you have ever seen the green in water that is forever flowing out to mystery and adventure then you know something of the colour of her eyes. I would not talk so foolishly but there is a space in me she steps into — a tall shadow, an absence that howls like a grave or a dead wind when she is not there. I am a fool for her, letting all of me be a mile-long night breeze if she is but a straw held up — a single golden hair I might rush over forever. I love Marsha Kirzner like the taste of my own spit, like my own blood in my veins, ready to melt in her heat like snow carried south and dropped in Pacific surges, my mouth dissolved in tropical mangoes and sweet papaya. She is another tall self I keep inside and lean on like a prop — a magic self that sets me whirling and dispersing — an anchoring self like a two-ton idol thin and heavy in the bed, me fastened to it like a small burnt lizard. Let me just hold this mantis woman in my arms, this tall beautiful fire with green eyes. Let me just lick the length of this green blade, this lightning filament of her love and I will sizzle with it, a long green furrow in my spirit where a jade lake reaches for the peaks. Her hand is a leaf that can calm the passage of a storm and yet it is a leaf that sings in its work like a reed made of human flesh, a musical flesh of gasps and sighs — a high sweet strand of water like a violin string. Aaaah draw the bow down again my loved one across the heart, across the soul, draw the bow down again and play forever the long sweet notes of our love.

ON HEARING THAT GANDHI TESTED HIS BRAHMACHARYA† BY SLEEPING WITH YOUNG WOMEN††

what was it like lying with Gandhi
while he tested himself
what was it like to lie down
at night with perhaps the
GREATEST MAN WHO EVER LIVED
and not get a little tingle —
a silver little jet of lust
somewhere, somewhere
in the testy northern Indian nights

God I love Gandhi
but I don't know whether I'd have wanted
him sleeping with my true love
though if she'd wanted to try "testing"
his Brahmacharya badly enough
I suppose I'd have no choice
"Come on" she'd say — "this is
possibly THE GREATEST MAN WHO EVER LIVED!"
and that would be it
I'd have nothing left to do but wish him luck
knowing already that he's a better man than I
who has never lasted the night
with her
yet

†a Hindu vow of celibacy
††as reported by William L. Shirer, in the book *Gandhi: a memoir*

THE CHILD CAME IN

the child came in from unexpected adventures —
mountaintops suddenly thrust up beneath him and huge rivers to
cross
he came in from wild africas of the night
where a continent of gulls moved over him on a savannah
where he had to wait
day by day for the arrival
of a caravan
or another boy on a bike, something to drag him
off
now he returns
from comets, from last stands
in the moonlight, the songs of crickets
a capella in the grass
he had been detained for questioning
something about a far-off planet
a secret river that flows through
night-time directly into boys
he came by black stallion
to a land of dogs, to a road where wild eagles lead
him deeper into a country of lions, straddling fences and rivers
the lianas were uncurling
there was a window opening up in a distant castle
and some young princess was just looking through right into his
eyes
when
the child came in
finally
bringing in a breath of twilight and danger
that his mother and i expel with relief
waiting for him to mount the stairs before we ask him

"Where on earth have you been?"

SINGLE FATHER

The father counts his money
then he counts his children
How many sons does he have?
He has one son
One Son!
The father counts the hairs on his beard
and does division
How many children does he have?
One child!
The father counts the windows
How many chairs in the house?
With mounting avarice he counts the chairs
How many? How many? How many?
How many fingers
He has ten fingers
How many children?
He has one child —
A son! A son!
but the son is gone
The father counts his shirts
How much sand does he own?
How many sons?
How many sons does he have?
Saturday the child comes to him
How many children does he have?
He has one
The man has one son
And how many fingers?
The son has ten fingers
"Good! Good!" says the father
grabbing his son's hand
as he comes in the door —
"So many fingers!"
"So many fingers!"

SPERM SPERM SPERM

sperm sperm sperm
sperm sperm sperm
aaah tugging the mad kites in the testicles
sperm sperm sperm
sperm sperm sperm

an armada of sluggish stars whir their halving fins
twirl their automatic propellers
we are sperm sperm sperm they would say
with their round white faces
just curls of information
we are genetic submarines
tender tender detonators
and if you think a man is lost, driven
imagine a sperm
only the halved makings of a man
only one instruction and motor
in row on row of coiled vegetal fire
springs of soul
dots of lust
all just waiting for a kiss, a sight, a tremble
to be melted down at once
into white willing wax
the heat-seeking sperm
waiting to get out and expand at the stars
tracking down something to get lost in
something to be complete in

PREGNANT WOMAN IN BATH
(The architect's lament)

what temple on earth —
the Taj Mahal, her round belly
the Parthenon, her long slender limbs
all sepulchres and churches, her flesh
her smallest finger, an eyelash —
no holy dwelling ever to be built on earth
can rival her beauty
in the bath
pregnant
and
30

THE ORIGIN OF "WOMAN"

Not woe to man
as I once thought
or even
Womb–Man
as the man-fastened
think
but
Womban
as in Terran
or African
or Canadian —
e.g.
a native of the womb
a
Womban

meaning all people
even men
are Womb-en
first

SLEEP POEM

I could be beside a thousand women
but I am beside you
I come down and lie beside the river
this is how stone sleeps, this is
how elephants sleep
  they come down all insomniac
and they listen to you
  soft river flowing
  they lie beside you and listen
and their breath calms down
and their heat calms down
lulled away by the rhythms
                  the currents
the mild winds, breathing
softer and softer
  bullrushes in your voice
breathing softer and softer
I could be lying beside
a cold mountain
I could lie by foreign forests
green with evening
I could lie by African lakes
deep in the motherland
close, close to the original
sleep
but I lie here —
  calmed by the sound
    of the stars
the deepness of the rivers
  in your dream
the countries are so vast there
and the love so true
  I want to walk there

with you immediately, I don't
need a talisman — it is your hand
I touch in my fear
I lie down beside you
night after night
like the pages of the calendar
  steeped in dusk
thick sleep syrup in all the veins
the eyes wide open
I lie down by you
as though beside a terrible black cliff
with black wings by
an endless starless sky
I lie down by you like a road
and float away
the cars carry me away, the sound of horns
fades away
the whir of wheels takes me away
like the sound of sails
your soft breathing blows me away
and when, like smoke the last tendrils
of mind are gone
the body, the dreamer
dreams

POEM FOR MY UNBORN CHILD

There will be a first time I will meet you
I have never seen your face
I have felt you kick, move around in your
beautiful privacy
have heard your heart like a frantic butterfly beating
beautiful and full of light
in there
the great pulse of the blood rushing through the veins
I have been frightened
startled by you
I have dreamed about you
and now I have felt your shape through your mother's belly
but I have never seen your face

yet I will love you all my life

HOMEBIRTH

coming down to a holy land
coming through the holiest domain
in a bedroom on bain ave.
elegantly believe me —
the room seems to pulse with shadow-circles
contraction rings about the moon
shuffling and shuffling
quietly with the right cries
the right sounds of anguish
pushing out this urgent passenger
freely into the world
two mid-wives and Jaylene
make a ring of magic
with their hands —
til
a milk-white bubble emerges — some fabulous jewel!
an amazing moonstone she has carried all milky
over fabulous borders to bring out here, aching and triumphant
what is this glowing crystal
she pushes
"It is good that your system makes such
strong membranes."
Eli, the four-year-old, saying —
"Push! You pushed me out
so you can push this one out too."
casual as though she were unearthing melons
a woman of crystal bringing forth a crystalline orb
a child within
then the bubble bursts shooting forth its amniotic milk
with an awful tear of anguish in her voice
she pushes again
and the brown flesh of the skull appears
amazing —

the shadows shimmer in circles round the room
the world is contracting
we are peering in in wonder
til another mighty shove brings the newborn head halfway
already breathing, through the widened ring of her vagina
unswallowing this tiny human
the head is out, another push — a miracle all of us gasping
this whole new being still attached to the inside
by a long white cord is out
slippery hot in my hands
all curled in instinct
a tense question mark
i carry terrified ecstatic
to her breasts
and wait

ON THE BIRTH OF MY SON

I am a mad butterfly, flying in a frenzy all around him, zappy and electric, my many colours going off like city lights as I whir and flap in and in, closer to him, calming down sometimes to a condensation, a drop of water he floats in, a gentle tear, a wave that bears him dancing around the house, little king, god-prince, little guru baby, taking it all in with such calm eyes til the next time you must grimace and fart or belch or hiccup. I am a stunned follower finally, an acolyte in some religion. Aaaah what it is to be a slave to a wish, a need.

NEW FATHER

She is a warm country of milk
and I am the black side of the moon
a burned out ship floating by

She is the shoreline to safety and I am
the circus — the whirling chariots
and frightening rides

In her arms he finds the great vales of his yearning
the country he will always belong to
I am a stranded province a wandering region

of music that sings madly near him
I wish I were a star like she is to him
but, for now I must be a crazy satellite

a little too large for the house
but near her and near him — near them

YOUR CRY

your cry is an opening in me
in my centre
in my trumpet-part
your cry is a bell in me
ringing with an awesome
emanation
crying for your mother
you cry for mine in me
and my father too would cry for his

your cry reminds me that there is a cavern
in me where winds howl
a kind of gasp, of the soul
a need-tympani
cold water drops on
splat-tapping
with a continuous cold beat
i don't know whether to be hardened to it
or tugged up to you immediately

the need for mother more desperate than thirst
to be cut from yourself at last — small flesh blob
in a barren universe
your cry reminds me that there is a mountain top in me
where frozen air runs wild hands of longing
over an insatiable agony
o mother, mother
maaaaaa shouts the baby boy
maaaa the deep tree intones aching to its roots
maaaaa cries out the twisted steel of wrecks in the snow
of streetcar rails and cold untouched balconies
his cry pulls the golden plug from my breast
and contentment leaks out in a wild black gust

so that i am a bronze shell again bereft of sunshine
when he cries there is only one thing for a shadow to do
to connect with that baby
to rush up to him, cooing, comforting
talking to yourself
and lift him, all needy into the cradle of my arms
holding him til he quiets down
til both of us quiet down
til his quietness is a quietness in me.

ODE TO THE MOTHER

Well into overtime
just as big men go down
and start to sleep
well into overtime
cry by cry
the great mother who made the men
who made the pyramids.
The mighty mother who birthed
and loved all the armies
and the generals and the dreamers.
This mightiest worker of them all.
For she is the support system
for the immobile and hungry infant
the government, the factory
the skyscraper of children.
She is the organizer and manager
of hostile properties
co-ordinator of juggled jobs
always on call, always going full tilt
too hardworked to lobby
for better wages
the work meaning more, trapped in the work
doing the work like Atlas, like Sheba
like Mother Theresa's mother.

I have a new perspective
on my respect for those who build stadiums
for those who gouge coal
from the bottom of the earth.

Let the steelworkers of legend
lay down their molten ingots
and take up for a while
a warm needing baby.

ROCKALONG

Whatever moves me moves you too
The wind on the earth
The sun and the moon
You lie in my lap dear
And here is my song —

When I rock you rock
You rockalong
When I rock you rock
You rockalong
Rockalong

Whatever warms me warms you too
The sun and the stars
The light of the moon
The wind to the eagle is singing this song —

When I rock you rock
You rockalong
When I rock you rock
You rockalong
Rockalong

Like a stone on a mountain
Like a drop in the sea
Like a voice in a choir
Or a leaf in a tree

Whatever soothes me soothes you too
The song and the sunlight
The wind and the moon
Soon you'll walk, one day you'll run but tonight —

When I rock you rock
We rockalong
When I rock you rock
We rockalong
When I rock you rock
We rockalong
Rockalong
Rockalong
Rockalong

Rockalong

GIANT OF THE COOKIE CRUMBS

When Charles Atlas lifted the mountains
my baby lifted up his eyes
and saw me
the horizon going over his head
like a forgotten umbrella
whole regions of sky hurled away from me
like a finally flung hat

As Charles held up the earth
my baby reached up his arms
to me
to stand
and I walked him
tall over towers
giant of the cookiecrumbs
through all the countries
of the house

MY SON'S HAND

It is a brand new van with those kind of sliding doors that close
with a longitudinal push and my first attempt has not quite
clicked it shut so I draw it back again for a firmer push. We are
waving goodbye. "Goodbye Peter. Goodbye Peter." But that is
not enough for my young son. He is too low to the ground and
can't be seen. He must peak back through the doorway — his
waving hand leading the way to that rapidly narrowing space.
"No!" The green door propelled by my thrust. The tender young
hand, slowly, slowly in microseconds moving to its moment, the
snap and catch, the click and howl. His little hand pinned,
bunched up like cloth — "NO" in the closed door. Staring,
disbelieving a moment at this grotesque echo from my own life.
Then, quick, the door is open, the shocked look spreading out
— holding him to me "NO!" Folding him into me. "NO! NO!"
These moments — true pain — "Can you move your fingers.
Can you move your fingers?" — before the little digits twitch —
before the little wrist bends. The hand unbroken! The elastic
hand fine but for a welt — a curved mark on the same hand —
the right hand — same shape, same place as my scar, almost one
on one. But he is recovered now — the hand forgotten in
moments of play-acting, the incident over but for that slowly
disappearing welt, written in his flesh like a letter in some
strange alphabet that finally explains everything.

PRAYER FOR MY SON

may your head be whole my son
despite the collision
may your great grey mind
still rest there clean upon the pages
you have loved so well
coming down like a beast to water
to read and loll there all day long
taking in Tolkien, Robert Jordan, Ursula LeGuin
all of them in long-abiding gulps, irritable to read
demanding to read
may your mind be well my son
it sits in the world like the top of a fuse
of miracle thought
amazing motion
dances we will unwind and do
together and apart
I must ask to put my blessing at your feet
to help you keep them solidly upon this earth

it was me who caught the foot
and lifted it too high
to bring you crashing down
Hephaestus to the ground
O god! may your brow be well my son
my genius son

DANIEL AGE 3

Daniel slips away
but he's still standing there
riding the blue wave
into a painting
into a story
or just a fantasy-thought
one more little cape
for identity to twirl in his
wild shaman's shuffle

O Dan who began with a smile
and then just smiled more

O Dan
who started with a laugh
and hit the highest note
I ever heard

PARENTAL HYMN

We who have been misunderstood
At last we must understand
Now is our time not to fail
Where we were failed
Not to hate where
We were hated
In our exile
We will be a home
Temple, and shelter
And in our sorrow
We must find the source of joy

It is with these most fragile things
That we will need our greatest strength
We have demanded everything
And now we must fulfill
We have been so selfish
Now we must learn
Complete devotion

TIME RELEASE POEMS

Words are magical that's why they must be spelled

❀

Sometimes it is the book
that opens you

❀

The teacher *is* the lesson

❀

If you would see a parent
look in the eyes of the child

❀

Home is where the heat is

❀

The last number is affinity
(Eli Kirzner-Priest — age 4)

❀

You can't make tea without water
(Marsha Kirzner)

❀

If an ice cream drops in the forest
and nobody cries
does anybody care?

❀

If a koan contains an infinite word
can it also have other words?

❀

When you own cheese
do you also own the holes in the cheese?

❀

Ice cream forever

✪

I said "ice cream"
not "ice cream"

✪

The sound of one hand
scratching you head

✪

Ignorance is blight

✪

A little bit of knowledge is a beginning

✪

A fool will always find
banana skins

✪

Are you ready for the euthanasia YET?

✪

Does a fool answer rhetorical questions?

RESURRECTION IN THE CARTOON

Here in the cartoon
resurrection is no miracle

Krishna, Christ, Lazarus
their risings are commonplace, profane
just a logical extension of the accident of death
usually humorous

The avatar cat rising up to face the cannon yet again
to be skinned once more by the escalator

There are no saviours in cartoons
no real redemption

Nor is there transformation
the duppy drawing springs back to life
always insanely intent
relentlessly pursuing
something quicker
smarter
than itself

And so we're dragged through the hoop
stripped down to some bone-self
the dumb button just jammed right in
automatic

The cruel karma machine
the wind-up cross, the electric man-hurler
I've come down on nails
on heads
on sticky stuff
an animated Hephaestus

still smelling of Aphrodite
still red with the raw hand of Zeus upon my back

I am hurled down repeatedly
a rubber Satan
a bouncy Christ
my features moving
so fast they distort
my feet on treadmill
my feet on insane

But I have power in the situation
I can run out over the edge of the cliff
and look, if I whirr my legs
for seconds
I don't fall

THE BIG FACE COMPETITION

The winners of the big face competition
are awarded face enlargements
by serious plastic surgeons

Afterward they are promoted to the B grant category
and put up against other former winners

There are no juries for these events
as the size of a face is an absolute
and determinable quantity

Everything from the tip of the nose
to the inner back lobe of the ear
is considered face
and remember it is surface that counts

Measurement is attained
by immersion in a tub or vat of lard

For application in other areas or disciplines
please contact Henri Offender
or his
little
knave

PARALLELVIS UNIVERSES

THE DEATH OF ELVIS 1

Elvis sat down on the toilet as big as Buddha and waited
it was the anniversary of his mother's death.
Elvis strained and his face went a little red
he thought of his mother dying that day
he had lost certain rights
he had become mythic in the mind
you lose so much when that happens.
Elvis strained again. He could feel something
moving in his centre.
Something really big.
Excited he pushed harder.
He pushed and grunted.
It was coming! It was coming!
Elvis strained until the purple veins stood out like
tree roots in his beet red neck
and then it came
bigger than Mt. Sinai it came
bigger than the first orgasm
like a deathstar spiral
the big black bolt shot through him
and Elvis keeled over
and groaned
a big fat man on the toilet
the sound of that last fart still reverberating
amidst the gasping
the crying
like any man dying.

ALTERNATE ELVIS REALITY A:)

Hideously disfigured
but at last anonymous again
Elvis
swept

ALTERNATE ELVIS REALITY B:)

Really happy about his new cunt
with the slow daily swelling of his new breasts
Elvis began to feel a fullness in his belly
such as he had never known
as a man

THE DEATH OF ELVIS 2

they went to get Jimmy Hoffa
but they got Elvis by mistake
that great voice wasted on the hook
that great vibrato ended with a boot to the throat
"I'm not Jimmy Hoffa!"
"I'm not Jimmy Hoffa!"

THE DEATH OF ELVIS 3
("THEY CALL IT ELVIS-LUTION" MOJO NIXON)

Surprisingly limber on his small toes, at home
in private, naked and very large, Elvis would dance.
There was no regret in his mind. He accepted each
new roll of fat with Buddhic glee.
It was not the svelte postal stamp Elvis that he loved.
He loved this new transformed Elvis.
An Elvis who had let a lot of stuff go
handsomeness
GULP! GULP! gone, bloated, distorted
that leer now, that sexual sneer just
a weird bit in the balloon that makes one whole
side of the face pull down in a slab askew.
But he cares not
for Elvis knows himself
he understands his soul-urge
and like a genius at home he can slink out
of his image-skin and be the man he is
giggling and jiggling with fat.
Like a young Santa Claus, Elvis
sits and rolls his rolls and laughs.
He plays his great hits and twitches
mocking his old self with lewd
self-accepting rudenesses.
Carnal Elvis. The evolved Elvis.
Able to leap quite high now and spin in the air
the big slap of those feet
as he lands ecstatic, sumo-like.
And Elvis is approaching the bathroom.
Yes, Elvis is approaching the bathroom.
It is the anniversary of his mother's death
and Elvis avatar is jumping and spinning wildly.
He has completely forgotten that he is Elvis Presley.
He is just a timeless bit of himself

soaring out towards the fated room
and alas, what might have been
if he had not just then landed
that delicate white foot on a bar of soap
and been upended, flipped over backwards. Smack!
Flop! On his great big belly
hard enough to bounce him halfway back up
and curiously, arse-first onto the toilet.
Already unconscious, the god-like head whips against
the supports of a shelf containing
ten round tins of spam.
These come rolling down one by one onto his head
until with a final THUNK!
the king is capsized from his throne
already dead
onto the bathroom floor.

YOU CALL ME KING

you call me king
you call me king
come see me on my throne then
come see my last judgement
come see my drugged noble lips slobber
in the death grin
i release it
i release it
a hardwire grin of mu metal
a metal that should
never be bent
or melted
or parted
a mouth not to be kissed
a hacksaw thing
a child thing
that used to sing so well
you call me king
you call me king

ELVIS/BACCHUS ITERATIONS

Elvis Bacchus, Elvis Bacchus
has no one else noticed the similarity
between these two names?
Say Bacchus 22 times using those precedents
of consonant decay over time
(as described by archaeologist
Colin Renfrew)
and Bacchus is Elvis

Listen:

Bacchus Bacchus Bacus Bakis Bekis
Mekis Mawkiss Nawkis Nawbis Nawlbis
Nelbish Nelfish Snelfish Stelfish
cellfish elfish elfis Elvis!

Elvis is Bacchus
Elvis in his prime
and Elvis in his decline
dead on the crapper
with a body full of drugs
Elvis is Bacchus
and Bacchus is us

TIME RELEASE POEMS

All drive no destination

☞

All icing no cake

☞

All grunt no pig

☞

Bowling the archetypes

☞

To burn a good cook

☞

To cut bread with a dagger

☞

To fear the gun and the butter too

☞

To break one egg on another

☞

To carry an egg in too many baskets

☞

All package no content

☞

All edge no interior

☞

To fall to your place in history

☞

To be attracted to magnets

☞

All interior no edge (infinity)

THREE DEVIL SONGS:

1 Little Right Wing Song Against The Victims

For too long we have blamed the crime
on the perpetrator

It's time to get the victims
in their bloody bandage disguises
they hide magnets in their throats
manipulating with their exploded hearts
the great issues of the world

Behind every great savagery I assure you
lies the hand of the victim
perpetually burning, sinister with portent
the victim conducts human electricity
forking it ever to the crime

the skinny excuse of being mangled
the great alibi that they are too young
the mere technicality that they have been silenced

2 Scapegoating

A skilful scapegoater like a diviner
Finds the hate-current in us
Draws it up through any branch any tree it needs

A scapegoat must be easy
It is important to pick a scapegoat you can hate
The whole lineage of

A scapegoat has to be available
Believable
There must be a construct a conduit
Some cultural *in* to the scapegoat

A good scapegoater will not seek the glory
Of scapegoating the brave, the bold or the protected
A good scapegoater will go right for the women and children

Imagine the air is hate
Now breathe in deeply holding the scapegoat in your mind
Don't push the scapegoat-breath
Let the breath build like a hill beneath the sands

3 Oppress the Oppressed

When times get tough
When the crime rate is high
When all the statistics show
That murder is on the rise
And spirit is down
More rapes
More little wars
Bigger wars.
When these things happen
We all know
The ancient solution —

Oppress the oppressed.
Put more of the oppressed in jail
More of them in smaller cells.
Beat the starved, slaughter the starved.
Take the starved to camps and brutalize them.
Degrade all humanity in the starved.

Like a jack in the box comes the answer
Like a bomb in the face —
Oppress the oppressed.
Gather them up and don't let them know
What's happening.
Examine their papers and meanwhile get them digging graves.
Get them back to reservations.
Give them disease and poverty
From general to general the bird of information hops
Dipping its bloody beak in deep again —
Oppress the oppressed.
Let there be longer jail sentences
More hangings
Let us ferret out single mothers on welfare.

We must cut aid to the poorest of the sick.
Times are tough.
We have to put our foot down.
Vote for the butcher!
Vote for the jailer and the general!
We need them because it is time
To oppress the oppressed.

TIME RELEASE POEMS

Bank robs man

❂

Ballads not bullets

❂

Christs of the cross-hair +

❂

Doom lens camera

❂

Executioner's overtime

❂

The cutback lumberjacks

❂

Confession hounds the liar

❂

He loves peace except among his enemies

❂

Be on my side
not on my back

❂

One candle lights another

❂

"Doom" is only "mood"
backwards

❂

Resolution not revolution

❂

The peace you make may be your own

❂

Not just PEACE but a JUST peace

❂

The only peace is JUSTICE

❂

Justice not justification

❂

We're bigger than all of us

❦

There is no balance without opposition

❦

I can see the planet in your eyes

❦

The only promise is doing

❦

I can't wait
to be patient

MODIFIED FAMOUS PHRASES*
(OR: BUTCHER SLOGANS NOT PEOPLE!)

If we can put a man on the moon we can
STOP THE WAR ON THE POOR

If wishes were horses beggars would
STOP THE WAR ON THE POOR

Don't pick your nose or your eyes will
STOP THE WAR ON THE POOR

Spare the rod and
STOP THE WAR ON THE POOR

It takes a lot to laugh but it takes a train to
STOP THE WAR ON THE POOR

Forgive and
STOP THE WAR ON THE POOR

To gain the world and
STOP THE WAR ON THE POOR

I liked this new stainless steel razor blade so much I had to go
out and
STOP THE WAR ON THE POOR

*This poem is intended for use at demonstrations. The leader
would call out the beginning of the famous phrase and the
others would respond with the modified ending. Other famous
phrases could be added, of course, and there might be many
more modified endings, such as "Stop ailments!" or "Ban
pesticides."

TEN REASONS

Because you probably won't be living here in a few years anyway
Because you're speaking on your own behalf
Because if they give you what you want
they will have to give everybody else what they want too
Because it's part of standardization
Because you have an agenda of your own
Because you're suddenly vocal
Because it wouldn't be fair to all those people who already had it
done to them
Because you're part of a special interest group
Because they've seen people like you before
Because you're one of those who scream loudest
Because you use every legal means at your disposal

HOW MUCH PATIENCE

how much patience does it take
to wait forever
and still get nothing
how much virtue in that
how many forms before you get the final
form letter of denial
a blank wall
uncrossable

how much patience does it take
when you are hungry
when you are angry inside
when you are going crazy
how much does it take
to finally get
the same old answer
as before

somewhere someone has got you by your children
got you by your organs
got you by the blood you need
or just plain food to eat
and you know clearly what must be done

how much patience does it take
to lie there bleeding
and watch it
not get done

WHEN YOU CALL SOMEONE DICKHEAD

When you call someone Dickhead
you refer to the glans penis, the frenulum
the super sensitive male penis tip
an almost supernatural part of the anatomy
almost a brain
almost another hanging heart

When you call someone Dickhead
you insult the wizened face
of who knows what hung
ancestor
in this vivid
wrinkle
this lifeboat
on the big tug

When you say Dickhead
drop the inverse reverence
you are bestowing a well-earned title
this grandest of all grandissments
should be reserved for those whom
we respect the most
popes, premiers, heavy metal singers
are Dickheads
because we are fair
because we respect the penis

MEDITATION ON A RULER

a ruler is very democratic
for it is divided equally
among its twelve inches
no one inch having more than another

and, as it is, thus, a tool
can be used constructively
or destructively
as when a master
slaps some erring schoolboy's hand

a ruler has an edge and a blade
it is like us in that it is divided
but unlike us in that each fragment
is not pitted against the other
nor does it inflict
with a plague of divisions
the world about it
but rather can be used
to join two sundered points
with a straight unerring line

finally
a ruler
when you hold it up against the sun
is unlike our cities and our politics
our bodies and the clothes of the poor
in that it is definitely made to measure

thank you

GO, GATHER UP THE LOVE

Go, gather up the love
I know now what we must do
It is in your eyes and my eyes
Go, and gather it up, look by look
gaze by gaze
one flame in a hand, one holy flame —
two flames gathered up —
Gather up the love in our children
Gather it through slum and hovel
through mansion and factory
with great gentleness, go
taking a spark here a glow there
turning down none of it
Gather it up and free it
if even just in your own lips
through your own heart
by being strong
by going always beyond your limits
Gather it to saturation
long past your centre
deeper than the full depth of you
Gather it up in beads
in blue flames, in fierce bonfires
Let there be a leap of love
in the centre of the earth —
a flame higher than the heavens
a leap of our commitment
of our will
a leap of fire
straight into the stars

IN THE NEXT WAR

In the next war don't drop the bomb
Drop the excess wheat
Drop the sacks of grain
and powdered milk we have too much of
Send our best men over
in daring flights
their bombers full
of fish eggs huge cheeses
and birthday cake icing
Don't machine gun our enemies
Rather let us scrape off our plates
and pelt them with the leftover squash
We must inundate them with sauces and gravies
each day a new and better recipe
We have the technology to do this
We have invisible aircraft
Now we must make an undetectable fleet
a holy sky train that drops a mountain
of Kraft Dinner and Coke
Bury the Kremlin in spaghetti
minute rice and mashed potatoes
This will be a new kind of war
It will take sacrifice and patience
Everyone will have to put something aside
for the enemy
Starting with the ham and eggs
saving for the very end
our big weapon
the hamburger

TIME RELEASE POEMS

Though the candle is crooked
the flame is still straight

❂

Sometimes the shadow is bigger
than the cat

❂

If you change either
you change the other

❂

Everything leads
to everything else

❂

Are you ready for the euthanasia
YET?
❂

It is easiest to fast
just after eating

❂

A dog abhors a vacuum

❂

Never tie a dog to your balls

❂

The knife will not soften
for the throat

❂

One tooth works with another

❧

Every tooth affects the bite

❧

Every turn of the wheel
sharpens the knife

❧

Every little drop
makes the rain

❧

If you want to bounce
you've got to hit the bottom

❧

You can't wait
for the "present"

❧

Just after the past
just before the future

❧

"Nowhere" is "now here"

❧

The day before the morning after

❧

People begin as dreams
and end as memories

❧

Without the void
we have nothing

❧

All are guaranteed an equal place in oblivion

❧

Longing for immortality
is always temporary

MESSENGER

running past the black cities
their temples dark against the stars
they are insignia randomly cast
everything has some meaning
there are motifs in the windows
each rivulet reads like a possible gospel
there is so much to be imparted
but all is in code
let me by: I am running in my sacred duty
I have been scrawled upon by god
look, there are rhythms in my stride
full of powerful information, incantations
formulae, there are exquisite proofs of innocence
enscripted in my flesh
please read me
please decipher
this whipped soundscape of skin
put the stylus to my fingerwhorls
that the world might know my song

for they have cracked the code of the wind
in any given face
and they can now know the exact articulations of water
as it exhales itself against a palm
your lips
all seem to be saying the same thing
please touch me
read this braille
surely there is some lost psalm in my flesh
please tell me what I say

POEM FOR RELUCTANT THREAD

yours is not to question
you are the thread not the tailor
you are the ship you are not the sailor
you must push yourself through
like a screwed up serviette through a donut hole
like a bag of beans through the effigy's eyes

all face
all piercing eyes
you must push yourself through
that's how you thread the needle
you give up your red reels of search unto the weaver
you surrender your long blue skein of yearning to the
seamstress
all now shall be taken by the frayed brow
and pushed inaccurately into tight situations
you are getting a hand

how beautiful you will be in tapestry
what a moment of red your own pure red will make
in the autumns of red woven there
you would push yourself through for this
in long gulping strands
in gallops of green
you are such perfect thread
you are haute thread
but you will come to nothing
unless you submit
to the eye of the needle

THE NEW OPPORTUNITY

This poem is not brought to you by Molson's —
but it was close, believe me
You see I had just done days of visualizations
asking for new opportunities
doing a vigil like a new knight
for this latest fad of cutbacks
when the phone rings
and its someone from an ad company
and they are doing a kind of
"spoken word" thing for Molson's
It will be subtle. It will be a poem
And at the end there'll just be a little
"presented by Molson's" kind of thing
"A poem?"
"A poem," they say
"And the client is asking specifically for you
but you will have to audition."
"No. I don't do that sort of thing," I tell them
"How much is it?"

It turns out to be a couple of grand
And maybe it's the beginning of a series of commercials
And if I'm the voice for all of them
Then we're talking more like 8000 bucks
Hmmm. Eight grand. And I've been asking the universe
For new opportunities. I'm being tested. I can tell
My stomach is clenched
So, what to do?

I have a family to support
I haven't had a B grant for seven years
I haven't had a works-in-progress grant for seven years
I've been living off the income from a song

And the income has dwindled down to oh so little
Just as the ultra right has taken over the government

Cutting grants and worse yet, cutting welfare
And introducing workfare
Eight grand over time is looking good

All the next day I agonize
I like beer — Upper Canada beer — not Molson's swill
But I won't actually be advertising said beer
I will merely be reciting some crap pseudo poem
I am being tested by the gods
But which way to go?

Every moment of the day hovers
Over which way I'll take this
How will it be to hear my voice
Emerge from passing cars
Betraying itself a 1000 times an hour
All over the nation
This voice I've kept so pure

And what if others recognize it?
What if Poet B hears it?
Poet C would surely hold me in utter contempt
for this one slip-up
Worst of all there's outright
outside revolutionary poet@.com
Is my reputation worth only a shot at 8 grand?
That's not even half a B grant!
"All you're doing is acting."
But the voice itself is sacred
No, matter is profane!
It is a test to see if you are in the world
This is the way the dirty world moves
And you are part of the mud

And the muck and the swill of the world
And you have a family to support
I'm almost at the sound studio now
But it could still go either way

I could easily get off the streetcar
At the next stop and just not show up
In fact I'm now half an hour late. Good
Even if I do show up (I've entered the building now.)
At least I've shown some disrespect

Fuck the world anyway
For making times so hard for a poet
This is what you get
Daintily now I'm approaching
Comfort Sound Studios.
I'm striding down a long hallway
To a door off the side at the end
There is the sound of chatter from inside
A smell of tobacco
I am nervous like a man about to make a speech —
Like someone who is going to be whipped
I round the last corner
And there in the waiting room
Are some people I know
Why it's poets B & C
Plus other poets
Poets I have never met
Poets I have always wanted to meet
Young poets
Old poets
I look around and even poet@.com is there
One guy looks sheepish
Others brazen unashamed
Most merely matter of fact
Resigned

After we all recite the pseudo poem
Written by an adman
Poet H
And I retreat to a local coffee shop
Where he tells me he is
The new poetry editor for a certain press
He wonders if he can have a look at my next book
This book

Aaaah
Opportunity!

Still
I wait till the next day
To call back the ad company

"Look, I'd like you to take
My name out of the running
For this one
OK?"

TO BE A MAN
(FOR CORIE, ELI AND DANIEL)

means living with the chemicals
nature creates to make you want
to procreate
you have to jive with absurd genetic systems driven to extremes
due to ice ages, famine, wolves, even women

instead of looking up from inside the bag
at the face of the one
who is holding the bag
you must now look down from holding the bag
at what is being held up
by you inside

a man like a tall tent pole
lifting to a peak a balance
of canvases and elephants
it is to walk around with your genitals outside
of your bones
without carapace or armour
to live upon the caprice of valve and pump
to be bloodbone
or pizzle
the absurd awaits
rife with perspectives

to be a man is to be a jellyfish in a lost tide
it is to be a little fleck of foam on god's exhausted lips
as he mutters endless imprecations on you
cursing every blessed bone and cell
sliver-keeper for divine deconstruction
you are a little of the shattered yang light
self-defining limitless
yet

born to be hemmed in
transforming
till your last edge extracts
itself from chrysalis
and lo what colours of being
arc above us in angelic artistry

IN MEMORIAM: ELLEN PRIEST

goodbye Ellen
how can you be dead
and England still there with all
its highlands and lakes
your wise eyes that lit up my early days
gone now — that much more smoke in the London air
London standing aggrieved
all its bridges black with your smoke
that rises at last free upon the breezes of this city
where you coughed your lungs out for years
the Thames like those long veins
in your legs

sweet Ellen the news saddens
three generations this side
of the ocean

so grandmother
with your gypsy blood
join your father and the generations
that cupped you or let you go
in the history now forgotten
now going on without you
with the leaves and autumn
and autumns to come all going
on without you
goodbye Ellen
who gave me my first knife
to eat with
a little knife
not sharp
but good to eat with
and had TV and chickens in the yard

so many times on your one visit
I framed you in memory
for goodbyes —
a side view of you in the back seat of the car
your profile against the moving window
that I will see forever
or touch like a piece of severed earth
from a land I love
mandala-like in the mind

even in your last days
you breathed the patriarch's black smoke
unable to use the common room at TV time
because some old codger was allowed to puff away there
coughing your guts out in that home
somewhere i'll not see now
living on so long
but gone now
2 months before my next visit

GRANDMOTHER

Goodbye grandmother
You were bigger than your life
You outlived the Thames and Walton
You outlived all the boys and men

You are old with novels grandmother
there are generations in this blue-veined skin
your old withered body a pulsing map
of what has been
what's come down
into the flesh
in this endless age
this age of credulity

Who made aeroplanes against the Kaiser
Who fed Canadian boys
in the Second World War
Who saw Queen Victoria's funeral barge
when she was two
go by her on the Thames

A drive that couldn't be turned off
even late into the nineties
when humbled by old age's
last instructive agonies
she could still do "Knees Up Mother Brown"
still play the piano
and flirt with young men

I shall never taste a mince pie so good
There will never be Christmases so good
as those generous Christmases
in your magnetic house

Thank you for those two rooms
from all four of us
Thank you for that first shelter here
in the frozen north

I can't believe
I will never see you
in this life
again

SONG INSTEAD OF A KISS

Song instead of a kiss
Darlin' this is a song instead of a kiss
To all of you who wait so long
On nights like this

Song instead of a touch
Darlin' this is a song instead of a touch
To all of you who ache who long
And need so much

It is to those who like to cling
It is to those to those I sing
Here is a song instead of a clutch
Instead of a moon
Instead of a soothing touch
In the afternoon

Song instead of a stone
Darlin' this is a song instead of a stone
To all of you out there alone
Who ache to your bones

It is to those who like to cling
It is to those to those I sing
Here is a song instead of a stone
Instead of the moon
Instead of a soothing touch in the afternoon

SOME VERY GOOD REASONS WHY

because it had roses caught up in it
beautiful jade roses
because of green eyes whirling
i married the tornado
because i live on the edge
ever running
and i loved the tug
the slow revolving
of the seasons round her
and the house she had captured
in her still centre
the house where the world whirled

because of complete surrender
because of cunt juice and roses
i married into
the long genealogy of the whirlwind
just for a spin
just for the centrifugal force
i wanted the blood to move to my back

i keep far from the centre of a woman
i ride the rim
she was right for me
for she could lay me down like a prairie
and soothe my miles and meadows
because she threw herself on my mountains
absorbing all my seas, my upheavals, my neural moons
she was sick of taking on the world
why not just one man
suck up his heart
his poems into her still centre

and just stand like that
wild inside
still inside
ever over kansas
ever under oz

IN SLOW APOCALYPSE

I love our moment in slow apocalypse
stretching out time
with tenderness or touch
and we speak fast here
in this crammed era
grateful for distortion
for digital
for the Doppler effect

just before the fall
the dance is most intense
a million moves a minute
scurrying to do
last things
meaning to build
more boats
grab someone and hold them close

rear back against the drift of images
let love flow against the age
offer our resistance
even in the detonator's mouth
we sing, we burn
to turn as slowly as possible
into fire and ashes

o raise a glass
to the flash
of slow apocalypse

IT IS THE INDESTRUCTIBLE

It is the indestructible in me
That longs for you
The strength
Not the incompletion
Whatever is whole in me
Wants you
Whatever is unfaltering
Wants you
I don't need you
To recreate my past
I want you because
I am new
And remade
Ready for what comes

I want you because
It is right for us
Because it is my freedom
To want you

SAFE RAGE WITH MATES

You have to direct your anger at the action
not the person.
You can say:
Your actions really anger me.
But you can't say:
You make me really fucking mad.
The words you make are incorrect.
They place you in the passive "done-to" stance.
The above statement should be reworded:
I get really fucking mad around (or at) you.

This pigpen in the kitchen makes me really angry
however, is an open statement.
It might still be you who allowed
the alleged pigpen to occur.
But don't curse *Pig!* under your breath
for this is to the person and offensive.
Why can't we communicate is not offensive
but so negative
so void of potential.
There must be potential even in safe rage.

I am really angry and I need to talk to you
is not a good enticement.
You should not yell
That's not yelling THIS IS YELLING!
If you have to yell
you must yell something non-threatening like
Don't be scared. I am only yelling.
It is very important not to make a fist.

As a bottom line
when the only words your rage supplies

are race/gender slurs, or suicide threats
it is currently deemed preferable and correct
to fall to the floor
and just shriek inarticulately.

A person shrieking on the floor inarticulately
has time out
the floor is a safe zone
the floor is off limits
and remember
you must not
bare your teeth.

IT IS NOT LOVE AT FIRST SIGHT

it is not love at first sight
that is the miracle
it is love at ninth sight
love at the end of the night
it is love the next morning
that is the miracle

TIME RELEASE POEMS

Down with slogans

❀

The only good slogan
is a bad slogan

❀

Honk if you hate your children

❀

Relax — and expect more terror

❀

To hide one calamity inside another

❀

To fear the cowards

❀

Taking pictures of cameras

❀

To love the smell of your own nose

❀

To fall on your own word

❀

Ventriloquism for Dummies

❀

Watch out for warnings

❀

Thou shalt not make commandments

❀

Getting rid of redundancy
because we no longer need it

❀

I'm looking forward
to looking back on this

❀

Stop procrastinating
tomorrow!

LOVE ANYWAY

I stole it from the Bible or was it the Koran
I heard it in the silence that came from a beaten man
I learned it at the bottom where the hearts get blown away
I saw it written on the wind
Love anyway, love anyway

I saw it in a vision that I had in infancy
It returned to me in a prison I made of secrecy
I tore it from a tender heart I broke along the way
I heard it from an unknown source
Love anyway, love anyway

Though the world laughs at you, fool
Though you've been castaway, betrayed
Though you could take the easy way out

I heard it from a woman veiled in mystery and power
I heard it from a tiny babe who only loved an hour
I learned it from the bitter cold and the merry month of may
I saw it in your green green eyes
Love anyway, love anyway
Sing those who've loved and lost
What more can I say
Love anyway

Love Anyway

lyrics by Robert Priest
music by Allen Booth

bi - ble   or   was   it   the Ko - ran,
vi - sion   that   I   had   in   in - fan - cy
wo - man   veiled   in   my - ste   and - power

I stole it from the
saw it in a
heard it from a

It   I re -

heard it in the si - lence that came from a beat - en
turned to in a pri - son I made of se - cre
heard it from a ti - ny who on - ly loved an

man   I learned it at the bot - tom where the
cy   I tore it from a ten - der I
hour   I learned it from the bit - ter and the

hearts get blown a - way I saw it writ - ten
broke a - long the way I heard it from an
mer - ry month of may I saw it in your

on the wind Love a - ny - way Love a - ny -
un - known source Love a - ny - way Love a - ny -
green green eyes Love a - ny - way, Love a - ny -

2nd 3rd

way   Though way
way

Though the world laughs at

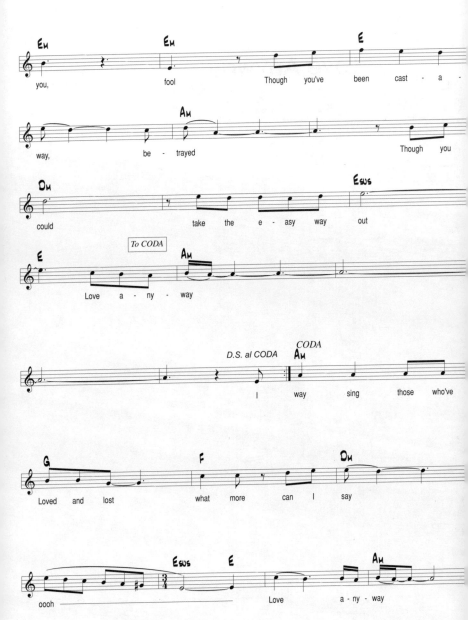

THE FUTURE OF PROPHECY

Astrology has long predicted its own downfall
There will be no prophecy in the future

They will develop a world-wide communication system that will
allow us to talk at any time to the person in the room beside us

First prepositions and then modifiers will briefly be outlawed by
litocracies on this continent

Buildings will own us in the future. We will be rented by rooms
Held by documents, rules will follow us

Don't worry Newtonian physics will continue to exert just
enough gravity
To keep us close to one another's throats

There will be rage drugs in the future
Berserker pills for the timid

Rage pill spills will pollute the ground water
The meek will go murderous en masse

Sure there will be pain but we will have such capacity for that
Our ability to experience agony will make a great leap

There will there be no darkness in the future
Darkness will be successfully obliterated everywhere —

Even under trees or inside rocks
All will be very well lit

SIP

Silence is cherry is lemon liqueur
You down a quarter ounce of liquid silence

You sip silence from the shadowy sherry cup
You bolt down sheets of silence when no one watches

You find silence in the place where you were seeking self
You come upon a vast silence like a field

There is silence in the bell, silence in the flake
Impacting on frozen grass

You go hunting for the beast, silence, but you find silence
Like a beast following you

GRAVITY

gravity of the situation
gravity of the emotion
each word has a gravity that draws your final word to it
you are alive with finality
without gravity there would be zero moment
laterally
there would be no motion down toward a disappearing point
all time is this — to make the space elastic enough
to snap back at the nothing
to whip the nothing with a towel's end of
talk

gravity of the dream
drawing the next dream down
dragging the next dream up
gravity at midpoint
at midlife

equipoise between the past
and the unpassing
gravity of the profane
events attracting other events
over vast distances, vast times
mortal gravity
gravity with shoes on
with trampolines

gravity of the lover drawing you closer
to the love
the love drawing you closer
to the light
the light drawing spirit
spirit gravity

dancing
spirit gravity
bringing
the blessing
ever closer
to the blessed

OSIRIS HYDREIS

i am a hill of fiery water
rearing up
above the valleys
if you nail me up
then i am a hill of fiery water on a cross
or if you bury me
then i am a hill of fiery water to the end
needing air
gasping
all fuel and flames
and a little piece of faith of face
of will to roll, to burn again for
this is the latest bubble in divine dentyne
once you're chewed enough
you can, again, for a while, have a fat moon face
and ambition
but if it were all god's breath, fine
forge on, I am ready to be remade, unmade, melted down
with every rapid exhalation
but there are gritty bits in my character
there are dead bit detonators that won't go off
i am not yet good gum
too crunchy
i am a hill of eviscerated water of dead water
of water full of drowned women, dropped babies
sunken moons
i can feel the longing to crush the coals within my breast
i can feel the urgency to squash the diamonds in my eyes
this glint of agony
unbearable
this flash of soul-stuff
right at you
scared shitless

i am a hill of trembling water
waiting to fall
into
my own resistance
oceanic
all
identity gone
o grant that the flood come to me

AN EXHORTATION TO DANCE

you have been taken to an office stretched out in a blue suit
by red elastics and extended into a painful alphabet-like shape
that you hate
    and we are asking you to dance
someone has cookie-cut you just as you are
you've always been like that — a brass monkey in the night
you've never leapt
you've never popped, hopped or bopped
    yet we are asking you to dance
some have been captured by clothing and forced to supplicate
caught up and ritualized
some have been standing like candelabras in the rain
for ten successive generations
unable to move til they are struck by human lightning
    well dance you strange shapes now dance pipes of
insignificance and elbow alphabets
    for too long you have lain beside the ocean on the sand
      spelling out the words "i need" with your limbs
for too long you have lain like a brand
like a rune of misery, heavy in the earth
the mark of a curse or a warning
you will say i have been asleep for ten million years
i have been beaten out of metal to make this shape
my limbs are fossilized in iron habits, ancient geologies
how can such deeply held oil dance
to which i reply with drum beats
    with electric guitars in ecstasy
  with wild sedimentary singing
    that breaks up everything in the heart
because everywhere you walk there is a shadow
joined to your foot like a refugee
and you have to drag around this darkness
until you lose it in the dance

so come and undulate your essences
    part being part not being
come and beat on the beach of brass again and again

  in moments of bubble time
  in moments of not knowing or knowing
    o come and be one
   come and be one
     of the many

BLUE PYRAMIDS

A Proposal for the Ending of Unemployment in Toronto

We should build pyramids on Yonge Street.
Cut blocks out of blue mountains in Collingwood
by traditional methods
and have them dragged here on logs
by the unemployed.
Pay them well.
Pay them $22.50 an hour.
This would get them back to work
at a wage they could buy houses with.
Build pyramids and then build houses.
From all over the world
they would come to see these pyramids.
What a tourist attraction!
Blue pyramids in Toronto!
and look —
people with houses!

And let there be good cheer too
about the building of these pyramids,
coffee breaks and full benefits.
Let the builders of the pyramids have OHIP
and daycare.
Yay, and I foresee ten thousand workers
gathered around a single blue block.
They sing the word "LIFT!!"
and it is raised into the air
on fingertips.
They march with it to Toronto
with people dancing atop it.

We should build pyramids on Yonge Street

and keep on building them —
great pyramids of peace to let the generations
wonder at.
What is this about unemployment?
We could end unemployment today!

You know and I know.
We must begin building
the blue pyramids of peace.

MEETING PLACE

someone spilled the whole spice packet
someone dumped the whole masala mix
someone toppled the whole smorgasbord
and there's so many of us
dancing in it
we keep brushing up against one another
rubbing one another raw
like sandpaper
shoulder to shoulder
lip to lip
we chip away at one another
like mutual sculptors

and the streets are so congested we often stand
pressed to one another for hours on hot humid days.
i come away my skin embossed with emblems
i have cross imprints in my chest
from some of you i get small fading secondary tattoos
impressions of scars that are not mine

i come home to find i've gone a bit buddhist
another day i'm slightly marxist
i dare say there are even days when i may get a little gay
we're all so close
we can't help tripping over one another
i jump up wearing your turban
you stroll off doffing my pope's hat
unknowingly we've switched destinies
now none of us can be responsible for lipstick smears anywhere
for the wind is full of colours
which were once ours — we inhale each other
we moosh each others' footprints
till all is one track

one common path through fast retreating snow

someone has emptied out the asylum
and the mad have all acquired black coats
we are lucky to be hosting a convention of local gougers
we are a dark assembly of international crows
a carnival of deposed dictators, disgraced premiers
and we've all been invited to the same dance

but who invited the poor?
the streets are full of evicted single mothers
we have hungry children of every nationality
so close i can't help but touch
and be changed by them

and i see that you are changed too
we both look a little deeper now
maybe we're taking each other somewhere
with this dance
i keep thinking we'll finally arrive
at something like justice in us

POEM* BROUGHT TO YOU

This poem brought to you by Pepsi
Brought to you by Blue
By Hilroy paper
This poem brought to you by Chrysler trucks
By Ethernet
Produced in association with the League of Canadian Pilots
This handmade poem typed by a famous Canadian craftsman
One in a numbered series of poems brought to you by Dunlop
Tires
Co-sponsored by Just & Mimic
To the ribbon makers
To the alphabet blacksmiths
No flies were hurt during the making of this poem
This poem has been approved by the council of fleas
This is a free form, unrhymed (as yet) list poem
Produced in part with a grant from the pork makers of Ontario
"They make better bacon"

*"Poem" is a trademark of BigFACE Music and cannot be used
without written permission

NOTES ON THE SONGS

The music for "Love Anyway" and "Rockalong" was written by Allen Booth.

"What kind of Voodoo" is available on my CD, Tongue'n'Groove (Emi/Artisan).

"Song Instead of a Kiss," as sung by Alannah Myles, is available on both *Rocking Horse* and her *Greatest Hits*.

Notation by Tom Leighton.

Chords Used in "Christ after Christ"
(Tune bass E string down to D)

Dm(add2) xxx23x
Dm9(aug5) xxx33x
Dm9(aug)/F xx323x
G/B x2xx3x
C(add2) x3xx3x